On-the-Go
FUN
for
KIDS!

On-the-Go **FUN** for **KIDS!**

MORE THAN 250 ACTIVITIES TO KEEP LITTLE ONES BUSY AND HAPPY— Anytime, Anywhere!

Amanda Morin

Aadamsmedia
Avon, Massachusetts

Published by
Adams Media, a division of F+W Media, Inc.
57 Littlefield Street, Avon, MA 02322. U.S.A.
www.adamsmedia.com

Contains material adapted from *The Everything® Kids' Travel Activity Book* by Erik A.
Hanson and Jeanne K. Hanson, copyright © 2002 by F+W Media, Inc., ISBN 10: 1-58062-
641-6, ISBN 13: 978-1-58062-641-5; *The Everything® Kids' Giant Book of Jokes, Riddles,
and Brain Teasers* by Michael Dahl, Kathi Wagner, Aubrey Wagner, and Aileen Weintraub,
copyright © 2010 by F+W, Media, Inc., ISBN 10: 1-4405-0633-7, ISBN 13: 978-1-4405-0633-
8; *The Everything® Toddler Activities Book, 2nd Edition* by Joni Levine, MEd, copyright
© 2012, 2006 by F+W Media, Inc., ISBN 10: 1-4405-2978-7, ISBN 13: 978-1-4405-2978-8;
The Everything® Kids' Geography Book by Jane P. Gardner and J. Elizabeth Mills, copyright © 2009 by F+W Media, Inc., ISBN 10: 1-59869-683-1, ISBN 13: 978-1-59869-683-7;
The Everything® Kids' Crazy Puzzles Book by Beth L. Blair and Jennifer A. Ericsson, copyright © 2005 by F+W Media, Inc., ISBN 10: 1-59337-361-9, ISBN 13: 978-1-59337-361-0;
The Everything® Kids' Crazy Puzzles by Beth L. Blair and Jennifer A. Ericsson, copyright ©
2005 by F+W Media, Inc., ISBN 10: 1-59337-361-9, ISBN 13: 978-1-59337-361-0.

ISBN 10: 1-4405-8920-8
ISBN 13: 978-1-4405-8920-1
eISBN 10: 1-4405-8921-6
eISBN 13: 978-1-4405-8921-8

Printed in the United States of America.

10   9   8   7   6   5   4   3   2   1

Cover design by Frank Rivera.
Cover images © Olesya Karakotsya/123RF and iStockphoto.com/FrankRamspott/mocoo.
Puzzles by Beth Blair and Scot Ritchie with additional illustrations by Kurt Dolber.
Interior illustrations © iStockphoto.com/senkoumelnik/Nenochka/FrankRamspott/
Jayesh/cisale/mocoo/jamtoons/loliputa/katyatya/ksenya_savva/AnMi and
Olesya Karakotsya/bloomua/Askhat Gromov/macrovector/ivook/Len Neighbors ©
123RF.

This book is available at quantity discounts for bulk purchases.
For information, please call 1-800-289-0963.

CONTENTS

Chapter 2: PLANES AND TRAINS 47

Chapter 3: HOTELS AND VACATIONS 71

Chapter 4: THINGS TO DO WHEN YOU'RE WAITING AROUND. 107

Chapter 5: SHOPPING TRIP GAMES 139

Chapter 6: BONUS ACTIVITIES FOR WORK-FROM-HOME DAYS 157

INTRODUCTION

As a parent, you probably spend a lot of time rushing to get kids out the door to that place you need to be *right now*. There are always errands to run, appointments to keep, carpools to drive, and vacations to get to. However, once you get out the door, it seems like you spend a lot more time waiting than you expected.

Fortunately, all you have to do is throw *On-the-Go Fun for Kids!* into your bag and you'll never have to listen to "I'm bored!" or "Are we there yet?" ever again! Throughout these pages you'll find hundreds of activities to keep your kids entertained whether you're waiting for your turn with the doctor, for your food at a restaurant, or for your family to get ready to start the day at a hotel. You'll also find activities to fill the hours in the car or on a train or airplane on your way to your vacation. And, since there will inevitably be days when your kids are home from school unexpectedly and you have work that needs to get done, you'll find a bonus chapter filled with activities that will keep them busy while you're busy, too.

Some of the activities throughout the book require you to participate or to gather a few simple materials to get your child started, but your kids will be able to do the majority of them on their own or with friends and siblings. With activities ranging from scavenger hunts, brain teasers, and word puzzles to apps, songs, and imaginative play, there's something in here to keep every child busy and entertained! You may even find yourself less worried about *getting* there right now and more concerned with *being* in the right now! Have fun!

Chapter 1

CAR TRIP GAMES

There's a lot going on during a road trip to keep your child occupied. But sometimes it's hard for kids (and parents!) to see those opportunities for fun while enclosed a small space for hours on end. Fortunately, whether you're driving cross-country or across your own state, this chapter gives you a number of ways to keep your child busy and entertained. From classic games like Road Sign Bingo to more inventive options like creating a custom license plate or billboard, this chapter is full of fun activities that are guaranteed to make your child forget to ask, "Are we there yet?"

Gas Station Count

Help pass the time before your first pit stop by asking your child to count all the gas stations you pass. As he looks, encourage him to call out any unusual names. There may be types of gas stations that your child doesn't recognize, such as various kinds of truck stops or local or regional companies.

If you don't see many gas stations, ask your child why that is. If he's not sure, throw out some things for him to consider. Does the area just not have very many people living in it? Is the highway you're on not a major route for trucks? There may not be an explanation, but it's good to get him thinking about the reasons behind such things.

What's in Your Road Trip Survival Bag?

You don't have to buy a lot of new stuff for your child, but some things are handy to have on hand during a road trip. Put them in a backpack if your child is able to reach it and unzip without help. If not, consider hanging a shoe organizer over the back of the seat in front of your child. That way he can reach for items and put them back on his own. Things to bring include:

- ★ Travel games with magnetic pieces (Keep in mind that small pieces can be a choking hazard for small children—pack accordingly!)
- ★ A deck of cards
- ★ Markers, crayons, and/or colored pencils
- ★ A drawing pad
- ★ Tape and safety scissors
- ★ Books or magazines
- ★ A calculator
- ★ Stickers
- ★ An MP3 player or tablet

CUL8R

Ask your child if she knows what a "vanity plate" is. She may be able to tell you that some drivers like to choose a combination of letters and numbers for their license plate that together create a message. She might also know that those plates look different from regular plates. Before you begin this activity, make sure you child understands that vanity plates give a message that will tell you about something the driver likes, what he does for work, or something about his attitude toward life.

Can your child correctly match the following people with their license plates? Give her the book and let her try!

HINT: If she's having trouble, remind her to try reading the plates aloud. Single letters can be used to represent a whole word. Sometimes numbers are used as part of a word. For example "CUL8R" is "See You Later."

US4EVR	BIG FAMILY	H82W8
	IMPATIENT PERSON	
XQZME	PATRIOTIC PERSON	IMFUNE
	FAMILY WHO LIKES TO SKATE	
SK8RS	COMEDIAN	5KIDZ
	POLITE PERSON	
	PATIENT PERSON	
TOTDOC	LONELY TENNIS PLAYER	10SNE1
	PERSON WITH BAD MEMORY	
I4GOT	PEDIATRICIAN	W8NC
	COMPUTER PERSON	
HRDDRV	MOM'S REMINDER BEFORE A TRIP	PB4UGO

What Would Your Plate Say?

If your child already knows how to read vanity plates, let her come up with a few of her own! Ask each family member to come up with some ideas for vanity plates that would fit their hobbies and personality. Write them down, then fold them up, and mix all the papers together. Then have each person take one from the pile to try to figure out what the plate says and who it would belong to.

 **WEB4U**

Does your child want to practice reading vanity plates before you hit the road? Check out this web site: *www.maine.gov/sos/kids/fun-games/vpgame.htm*. She can guess what these vanity plates from the state of Maine mean—and check to see if her answers are right!

What's Your Plate Worth?

When your child gets tired of thinking about the words and letters on license plates, it's a good time to start looking at the numbers. Ask your child to pick, at random, a license plate he sees and to write down the number. If he adds all the numbers together, what's the total? Is that number more or less than the next plate he sees?

If he gets stumped because the license plates have letters in them, don't worry! You don't have to teach him algebra just yet! Instead, he can use a common substitution code to turn the letters into numbers. All he has to do is assign each letter of the alphabet a number. For example, A=one, B=two, C=three, and so on.

DESIGN A LICENSE PLATE

As you're traveling, you'll see many different types of license plates, and your child may notice that states sometimes change the designs of their license plates. For example, Maine has the state bird, the chickadee, on its license plates. But until 2000, all Maine plates had lobsters on them. In addition, some states also have special designs for veterans or to show support for certain causes, such as breast cancer or autism awareness. Sometimes a state may also change the slogan on its license plate.

Challenge your child to come up with his own slogans and designs for different states' license plates. His slogans don't have to be serious; they can be goofy or silly, too. The same goes for the design.

Remind him that on real license plates, the colors often will have something to do with the state's geography or its famous places (like green for a state that's known for all its forests). But this doesn't have to be true for his design. He could draw a joke license plate with a picture of the hotel you're staying at and a slogan like "The rain-soaked state," if it was raining while you were there.

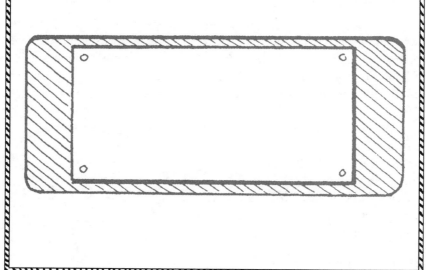

License Plate Delight

When you're in the middle of a state, any state, take a half an hour and have your child count the number of license plates from the state you are in and the number of plates she sees from other states. How do they add up? Once your child is done counting, ask her how she thinks the numbers will change when you are driving near the border of a state. What are the results when you are driving in a city? Ask your child to count again as you get closer to the state border. Are the results different from the count in the city?

TECH IT UP A NOTCH

State Plate Bingo

This app helps your child keep track of the license plates she's seen without having to write them down. She can also learn facts about each state. Once she's seen a license plate from a certain state, she can enter it in the app and that state will change color on the map. (iOS)

Are We There Yet? Tickets

If you're like most parents, you're tired of answering the question "Are we there yet?" Thankfully, this activity takes the mystery out of what "soon" actually means! Divide your trip into half-hour segments (or fifteen-minute segments for the younger travelers). If you're driving through areas with heavy traffic, you may want to divide the mileage instead.

Use slips of paper to make tickets for each segment and tell your child how many tickets it will take to get there. As each fifteen-minute block of time passes, hand your child a ticket. When she's collected all the tickets, you should finally be at your destination!

Are we there yet?

BIG CITY WORD SEARCH

If you're driving through the city and need something to entertain your child, just pass him this puzzle and let his surroundings inspire him. In this word grid, see if he can find sixteen things he might spot when driving through a big city. The words can go backward, forward, up, down, and diagonally.

BUS STOP	HOTDOG CART	RESTAURANT
CITY BUS	MALL	SKYSCRAPER
COFFEE SHOP	MUSEUM	STREETLIGHT
CROSSWALK	NEON SIGN	TAXI
CROWDS	PHONE BOOTH	
DINER	POLICE	

```
P D C R O S S W A L K S M
R O I T O K Y O J A T U R
E P H N A M A L L R S N E
S S N S E H A S E E P P
T U O I E R V E U O E O A
A B R X T E T M N W E L R
U Y N A T L F S Y S I I C
R T X T I M I F D I L C S
A I L G I G O N O W P E Y
N C H E N O P L E C O I K
T T N I P O T S S U B R S
P H O N E B O O T H T W C
O W O T R A C G O D T O H
```

Extra puzzle points: After your child has circled all the listed words, have him read the leftover letters from left to right, and top to bottom. He will find a fast fact about the world's largest city!

TECH IT UP A NOTCH

Geography Drive USA

This app will help your child learn about the United States. It has map identification games and trivia questions about the states. There's even a virtual visitor's center where your child can read informative brochures about each state. Your child's correct answers earn him "money" to "buy" gas and other things for his virtual car. (iOS, Nook)

Colorful Cars

There are plenty of interesting things outside the car windows that your child will pay attention to while you're on the road. And there is a wide variety of colors to be on the lookout for, too. Ask your child to keep track of how many red cars he sees in five minutes. How many green ones does he see in the next five minutes? What color car does he see the most of? For example, are most of the cars on the road blue?

VARIATION ONE

Once your child is warmed up, challenge all the passengers to find a rainbow of car colors. The catch is the rainbow needs to be spotted in color order—red, orange, yellow, green, blue, and purple. And once someone says, "Red car!" nobody else can claim the same red car. To make this game even more challenging, try playing the game with the rule that trucks and buses don't count. The first person to see all the colors of the rainbow wins.

VARIATION TWO

Make the game more challenging for an older child by asking her to find cars in shades of colors. Can she find a light green car? What about maroon, silver, or sea-foam blue?

BRAIN TEASER:
CAN YOU COUNT THE LEGS?

Test your child's brain game by asking him the following brain teaser!

Joey and his sister Hannah like to play "I Spy" when they travel in the car. They decide that this time the first person who "spies" the most legs on the trip wins! Joey sees two deer, eleven cows, two cats, and a spider. Hannah sees one turkey, seven cows, three sheep, and four cats. Who won?

PICKUP TRUCK

Tired of talking? Give your child this puzzle in exchange for five minutes of in-the-car peace. Have her start at the letter *B* marked with the white dot. Follow the truck clockwise around the wheel picking up every third letter, then write that letter on the lines provided. When she has finished, she will find the answer to this riddle: Why are sleepy people like automobile wheels?

Why are sleepy people like automobile wheels?

_ _ _ _ _ _ _ _

_ _ _ _ _

_ _ _ _

_ _ _ _ _ !

Speeding Down the Highway

If you spend a lot of time driving in the city or the country, your child may not be used to watching people drive on the highway. As you know, people can drive strangely on the highway, and their behavior can be due to the posted speed limit signs or the flow of traffic on the highway.

Have your child keep track of the posted speed limit signs, then ask:

◆ Are there noticeable patterns about when the posted speeds change? (For example, the speed limit may be lower when the highway goes through more populated areas or in areas where there are many animals crossing.)
◆ Why do people keep switching lanes? (Usually it's to pass other cars or to let other cars pass.)
◆ If you're driving the speed limit of fifty-five miles per hour and your destination is sixty miles away, will it take you more or less than an hour to get there? Can your child explain why?

Once your child has had a chance to examine highway driving, you can discuss what he's learned. Does he have any theories as to why people prefer highway driving to driving on back roads? (You may want to ask him to consider how the speed limit might play into the answer.) He may also have a better understanding of why some people find highway driving more stressful than driving around town!

BRAIN TEASER: HOW DOES X MARK THE SPOT?

Test your child's brain game by asking him the following brain teaser!

When Bill added 5 and 5 together, his answer was an X. How can that be?

BEEP, BEEP

The Dot family has spent the day at a giant amusement park. Now it's time to go home, but where is their car? Look around carefully—Papa Dot had it painted a special way, and even got a special license plate. Can your child spot the Dots' car, and find the family a path to it?

 START

Funny Business

One of the things that helps a business is having a clever and unique name—that way, people will remember it. Ask your child to keep track of the stores and businesses you come across in your travels. How many of them have funny names? How many of the names are funny on purpose and how many just sound goofy when she says them?

See if she can find business like "Sue's Shoes" or "The Sew What Fabric Shop." She could even make a list for your whole trip.

If your child were to start her own business, what kind would it be? Maybe the signs and businesses she sees on your trip will help her with ideas of her own!

Your Car's Name Is Special

Challenge your child to count the number of words she can make from the letters in your car's name. For example, if you have a Nissan, she could probably start with "is," "an," and "sin."

To make the game a little harder for your older child, challenge her to do the same thing using the make *and* model of your car. She could even try to make silly sentences. The sentences don't even have to make sense. For example, if you have a Nissan Maxima, she could make the sentence, "Six mamas in an . . . "

When she runs out of ideas with your car's name, she can do the same thing for each of the names of the people in your family.

TECH IT UP A NOTCH

Q Road Trip

This app is very simple. It just asks questions for your whole family to answer. Some of the questions are funny, while some are designed to make you think harder and to learn more about the people you're traveling with. (iOS)

COUNTRY ROAD WORD SEARCH

If you're driving down a country road and need something to entertain your child, just pass him this puzzle and let his surroundings inspire him.

In this word grid, see if your child can find fifteen things he might spot when driving down a country road. The words can go backward, forward, up, down, and diagonally.

BARN	GARDEN	POND
CHICKENS	GAZEBO	SILO
CORN FIELD	HAY WAGON	TIRE SWING
CROW	OLD DOG	TRACTOR
FARMHOUSE	PICKET FENCE	WOODPILE

```
E  T  I  R  E  S  W  I  N  G  B
T  C  T  R  A  C  T  O  R  A  O
E  W  N  G  E  T  W  O  R  C  S
S  O  G  E  T  O  O  N  O  G  N
U  O  A  T  F  L  H  R  E  O  E
O  D  Z  O  I  T  N  T  P  D  K
H  P  E  S  H  F  E  O  E  D  C
M  I  B  R  I  S  N  K  I  L  I
R  L  O  E  D  D  E  ☺  C  O  H
A  E  L  G  A  R  D  E  N  I  C
F  D  N  O  G  A  W  Y  A  H  P
```

Extra puzzle points: After your child has circled all the listed words, read the leftover letters from left to right, and top to bottom. He will find the answer to this riddle: Why did the chicken cross the country road?

Cars: Name It Time

How many different makes and models of cars do you and your child know? Show off your knowledge with this round robin game! In the first round, each person says the name of a car company (sometimes known as the make). For example, you might say "Lexus," and the next player might say "Ford." Keep going until you can't think of any more car companies, then move on to listing models, such as "Ford F150," or "Subaru Outback."

VARIATION

Add a twist to the game by allowing players to name makes and models that don't really exist. The other players have to guess whether it's real or not. For instance, did Ford really have a Model B+?

BRAIN TEASER: WHICH DOESN'T BELONG?

Test your child's brain game by asking him the following brain teaser!

What doesn't belong? Snow skis, Jet Ski, bus, motorcycle.

Higher Math, with Paper

Your child can keep track of how your speed changes as you leave the highway by making a graph. Choose a time when you're transitioning from straight freeway driving to an exit ramp. For five minutes, tell your child the speed of the car every minute (by your watch). Then she can make a little graph to show how the speed changes.

All she has to do is draw a little ladder, with a higher rung for every ten miles per hour slower. The bottom line of the graph can be measured in minutes. As you tell her the speed at each minute, she can put a dot for how fast you are going. By the time you reach the end of the exit ramp, she should have a descending line to match your decreasing speed.

Miles per Gallon Math

The next time you stop to fill your gas tank, reset the trip meter (usually beneath the odometer) to zero before you leave the gas station. At the next stop for gas, have your child check the trip meter to see how many miles you have gone. Then, have her write down the number of gallons of gas you just put in the car to fill up again. (The number is usually on the pump's gauge just below the amount you paid for gas.) That will tell her how much gas you have used since the last fill-up. Now she's ready for the real math!

Have her divide the number of miles on the trip meter by the number of gallons of gas you have used. (If she's stumped by doing it on paper, she can always use the calculator on a smartphone or tablet.) The result is the miles per gallon. If the number she gets is especially high or especially low, it could mean that you've been driving in the country with few stops or few slow-downs (which results in really high gas mileage), or in a city (this results in really low gas mileage). It's more likely the number will be somewhere in between.

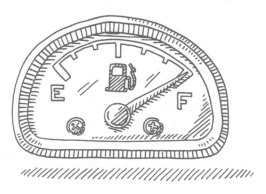

Share This Fun Fact

The gas that makes your car go is mostly oil, which is made up of the decomposed bodies of plants and animals that died millions of years ago. Over the years, their bodies have been smashed under thousands of feet of mountains, thick layers of dirt, even the ocean's floor. Gasoline is really just made of squished-up fossils, which is why it's called a "fossil fuel."

PIT STOP

Whether you're traveling to a city, through the country, on the coast, or up a mountain, there is one thing you'll need to stop for almost everywhere you go. Tell this to your child, then hand him the book and a pencil, and have him connect the dots to solve the riddle.

You gotta get

Mileage Math

Does your child know how to convert miles to kilometers? (Every mile is equal to about 1.6 kilometers.) When you pass the next road sign that gives the distance to the next city or exit, see if your child can convert how far away it is in kilometers.

Hint: She has to multiply the number of miles by 1.6. For example, 20 miles would be 20 × 1.6, or 32 kilometers.

Your older child might even be able to take on the challenge of converting kilometers back to miles! Convert it yourself (either on paper or by using your smartphone or tablet), tell your child how many kilometers it is, and then see if she can tell you how many miles.

Hint: This time she needs to know that each mile is .6 of a kilometer. That means she needs to multiply the number of kilometers by .6. For example, 30 kilometers would be 30 × .6, or 18 miles.

Billboard Alert

Have your child count the number of billboards she sees and pay attention to how they change as you go from area to area. Are city billboards different from rural ones? Are there some states in which there are no billboards at all? If your child says no, you can tell her there are four states in which billboards are illegal! (Vermont, Maine, Alaska, and Hawaii)

THE FIRST BILLBOARDS

Once upon a time, there were no billboards.

The very first billboards go back to the 1830s and were used by circuses to advertise their shows. Much later, from 1925 to 1963, "Burma Shave Signs" became a regular sight along the highways because they all advertised the same shaving cream, called Burma Shave. Every sign was red and white, and displayed a line of a rhyme. They were small, only about two or three feet long and two or three feet wide, and usually came in groups of five signs. The signs were maybe twenty yards apart or so, in a line along the side of the highway. Almost none of these rhymes had anything to do with shaving cream, and none had pictures, but they caught the attention of drivers, which is what was important.

See if your child can create a new product with a catchy name to put on a billboard or a series of road signs. He can think of a cool slogan for the product, or come up with an image or scene that would sell it without using any words. Remind him to think about the size and colors of the letters and words. After all, if he wants to sell something with a billboard, he'll have to grab people's attention in a split second. Have him ask questions like, "How can I get a person who's driving or walking by to notice the billboard for my product?" or "What makes a billboard stand out?"

Once he's formulated his idea, hand him the book and have him draw out his billboard in the following image:

BATTY BILLBOARD

Driving along you will sometimes see an old billboard that has lost a few letters, which makes the message left behind difficult to read. Give your child this puzzle to see if she can fit the fallen letters and missing word fragments back into this billboard so she can read the message.

```
_RAD__    _OB'S BIG
   HO_   _ LE
 _HIS ___RED__LY
SUP__ SA__ W___
ON__ LAS_ A VE__
    __ORT TIM_.
 _HOP _OR _HOE_
    —  _OW!
```

S E F A I
T L N RY
B E E
INC S ER LE
IB LL S LY
T SH S ER
ER

Window Art

If you don't mind having to clean the rear windows after a car trip, invest in a set of window markers or bring along some dry-erase markers for your child. She can doodle or write messages on her window while you travel. For some added entertainment, she can use inexpensive stencils to create a thematic window scene.

Car Rhymes

It may go without saying, but don't forget that young kids love to rhyme. Ask your child to come up with all the words he can that rhyme with "car." Remind him that these words can be more than one syllable, like "OnStar." Other words include:

- tar
- star
- scar
- crowbar
- cookie jar
- candy bar
- far

BRAIN TEASER: CAN YOU FIND THE DIFFERENCE?

Test your child's brain game by asking him the following brain teaser:

What's the difference between 124 and 12?

Road Sign Bingo

Does your child pay attention to all the different road signs as you travel? Check out this website from the Department of Transportation in Washington State: *www.kingcounty.gov/transportation/kcdot/Roads/ TrafficMaintenanceEngineering/TrafficSignBingo.aspx*. Before you hit the road, you can download Road Sign Bingo cards to take on your trip. Your child can learn what the signs mean before you hit the road and then keep his eyes open for them. When he sees a sign that is on his card, he can mark it off (and if you're not driving, you can play, too). Bingo is an especially good car trip game because there are so many ways to win—create an *X*, fill in one row, or even filling in the whole page!

VARIATION

Make the game a little more challenging. When you see a road sign, don't point it out to your child. Instead, tell him you just saw the sign that stands for "merge." Then he has to remember what that sign looks like in order to cross it off on his card!

TECH IT UP A NOTCH

Road Trip Bingo HD

This app allows more than one player to have a travel-themed bingo card and to compete to see who fills it first. The cards show up on the screen of only one device, so if your child isn't good about sharing, you may want to go with the single-player version of Road Trip Bingo instead. (iOS)

PRETTY POSTCARDS

If your child is tired of just watching the scenery go by and needs some additional entertainment, just pass him this puzzle and let him dream about the places you've seen. Sonja is driving with her family from a vacation in Maine back to her house in California. On the way, she stops in eighteen different states. At each stop, she mails a postcard with the state abbreviation on it. But the postcards don't arrive at Sonja's house in order from Northeast to Southwest! See if your child can plot Sonja's trip on the following map. He can shade in each state as he puts the postcards in order from Maine to California.

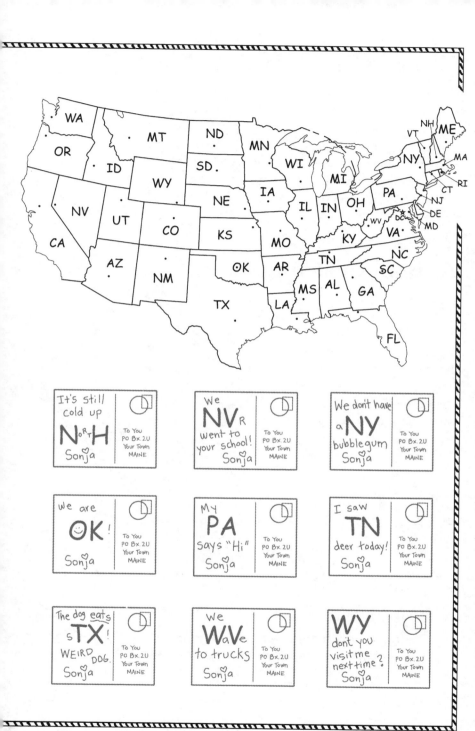

It's still cold up NoRTH
Sonja ♡

To You
PO Bx. 2U
Your Town
MAINE

We NVr went to your school!
Sonja

To You
PO Bx. 2U
Your Town
MAINE

We don't have a NY bubblegum
Sonja

To You
PO Bx. 2U
Your Town
MAINE

We are OK!
Sonja ♡

To You
PO Bx. 2U
Your Town
MAINE

My PA says "Hi"
Sonja ♡

To You
PO Bx. 2U
Your Town
MAINE

I saw TN deer today!
Sonja

To You
PO Bx. 2U
Your Town
MAINE

The dog eats sTX! WEIRD DOG.
Sonja ♡

To You
PO Bx. 2U
Your Town
MAINE

We WaVe to trucks
Sonja ♡

To You
PO Bx. 2U
Your Town
MAINE

WY don't you visit me next time?
Sonja ♡

To You
PO Bx. 2U
Your Town
MAINE

Keeping Track of Your Track (GPS)

If you have a tablet or mobile device that your child can use, let her follow your road trip route with a GPS or map app. Help her program your route into the app, including the stops you'll make along the way (if you know them). She can follow your progress. And, as long as you have 4G LTE, your child might even be able to research the best restaurants, tourist attractions, and other interesting information about your next stop.

Some GPS apps even keep track of traffic patterns and roadwork, so your child can have a sense of when you might get stuck in traffic!

Animal Crossing Alert!

Has your child ever seen those yellow caution signs that warn motorists of animal crossings? Brainstorm with your child some of the animals he might see crossing the road and then see if he can draw the "Animal Crossing" sign that would go with them. Depending on the animal, he may come up with some crazy looking signs!

BRAIN TEASER:
HOW CAN YOU SEE THROUGH SAND?

Test your child's brain game by asking him the following brain teaser!

The class was really puzzled when the teacher asked:
"When can you see through the desert?"
Do you know?

TRASHMOBILE

Does this look familiar? These kids have been in the back seat too long—you can tell by all the stuff they have piled around them! Hand your child the book to see if he can find the following sixteen items hidden in the mess.

Capital letter F
Diamond ring
Dog's head
Fish
Jack-o-lantern
Key

Needle
Pencil
Postage stamp
Sailboat
Scissors
Snake

Teapot
Toothbrush
Two slices of pizza

Farm Animal Fun

Pointing out cows and horses on the side of the road can get tiresome on a long road trip. Make it a little less boring by making it into a game. Whenever you pass a farmhouse, you and your child (if you're not the driver) or your child and a friend or sibling should count the number of cows, horses, and other animals they see on their side of the road. The person who has the highest number at the end of the trip is the winner.

VARIATION

Think about assigning each type of animal a point value to make the game more competitive. Here's an example of how to do that:

- ✦ Black and white cows = one point apiece
- ✦ Other colored cows = two points apiece
- ✦ Horses = twenty points
- ✦ Horses in groups of more than one = thirty points per horse
- ✦ Chickens = one half point apiece
- ✦ Barn = twenty-five points
- ✦ Hay bales = forty points apiece

If, for some reason, you're traveling through an area that seems to have more cows than any other farm animals, that's okay. You can use things like streams, bridges, or rock walls as substitutions in your point system.

What's Going on with That Car?

Have your child choose a nearby car and then each make up a story about who is in it, where it's going, and where it has been. Point out to her that there are clues she can use to develop her story. For example, a minivan is more likely to be a family vehicle, and the people in a car with luggage boxes on the roof might be moving or going on a long vacation.

Tell each other your stories. Then you can each guess what stories other people might tell about you based on *your* vehicle!

WHAT DOES THIS STAND FOR?

Once you've been driving for a while, your child will probably figure out that the letters "MPG" are an acronym for "miles per gallon." Hand him the book and ask him to figure out what the acronyms in the following pictures stand for.

SOS

SWAK

S _____

O _____

S _____

S _____

W _____

A _____

K _____

Punch Buggy

This classic car game never goes out of style. The rules are simple. In this game, the first person to see a Volkswagen Beetle (a VW Bug) on the road shouts "Punch Buggy!" (You can decide whether your family wants to add the classic punch in the arm that usually comes with it.)

VARIATION

Padiddle is a game better played at night or on a rainy day. The object of the game is to find cars that have one headlight burned out. The first person to see one has to yell, "Padiddle!" and tap the ceiling at the same time. Each Padiddle is worth a point. If a player is mistaken about seeing a Padiddle or it turns out to be a motorcycle, he loses a point.

ON THE ROAD

Your child has probably noticed that there are a lot of different kinds of vehicles on the road, but has she paid attention to how different these vehicles actually are? See if she can puzzle it out in this crossword. Explain that she can use the small pictures as clues, and then fill this puzzle with the names of some familiar vehicles that you might see as you travel around. We have left her some V-R-O-O-Ms as a hint!

License Plate Silliness

Choose a license plate and say the letters aloud. If the plate is only numbers, you'll have to choose another one. Ask you child to come up with a silly phrase using those letters. The sillier the phrase, the better. For instance, the letters *CWS* could stand for "cows with shoes" or "chewed worm sandwiches." When he can't think of more phrases, choose a new plate.

TECH IT UP A NOTCH

Road Trip Scavenger Hunt

This app is a high-tech version of a classic road trip game. Your child can enter in the names of all the players, decide what you're hunting for (words, items, or both) and choose how many points it takes to win. The app then randomly chooses something you all have to look for. Just click on a player's name to indicate he's found what he's looking for and the app will keep score. (iOS)

Doing the Wave

Are you stuck in traffic? Challenge your child to cheer up the people in nearby cars by trying to get them to wave at your car. Let her know that as long as she's polite about it (no mean faces, inappropriate comments, or rude gestures), she can do whatever she can to get a wave. She may want to smile, pout, wave, make goofy faces, or even hold up a sign that says, "Please wave! It will make my day!"

Touch Blue

This activity is a more sedate version of Twister that your kid or kids can play in the car. You take on the role of leader and call out a different color for the player or players to touch with their hands or feet (for example, "right hand, green!"). Each player may touch something nearby that is within reach, including each other's clothing. The game ends when the child can no longer reach or find the color that you call out.

Map Magic

Before you leave on your trip, help your child map the route on a site like Google Maps. He can add the landmarks you're planning to see on the way, print the map, and use it like a treasure map. As you get to each landmark, have him mark it off on the map. You may even want to consider letting him buy a small souvenir or postcard so that X really marks the spot where he finds treasure!

VARIATION

Have your child draw his own version of a map. Using a large piece of paper, have him draw your house at the start. Then he can draw the roads and pictures of the things you'll see along the way. You might be surprised by what he thinks the Statue of Liberty looks like!

Dancing Statues

This in-the-car game will help your child develop listening skills and will give you a few seconds of peace and quiet during your car ride. When it's not your turn to drive, turn up the radio or play a song on your MP3 player and encourage your child to dance. Of course, she'll have to be creative since she's sitting down and has her seatbelt on! Then, randomly stop the music and ask your child to freeze and hold her pose. If she moves, she's out and the game begins again.

To mix things up, ask your child to hold her pose for longer amounts of time or turn the music on and off quickly to throw her off her game.

GO! GO! GO!

When you're a road trip, you and your family probably find yourselves constantly on the go—which makes sense! You always want to rush to get somewhere fun and then take your time getting back. If your family is in a hurry, pass the book to your child and have him see how quickly he can travel through the following list to fit all the letter sets into their correct spaces.

BYE	LD	IN	T	ORE
N	WN	N	LA	OD
DI	AMI	CA	CHI	WA
N	LE	BB		
FOR	RIL	DRA		

Not silver = <u>G O</u> _ _

Long dress = <u>G O</u> _ _

Turkey noise = <u>G O</u> _ _ _ _

Large ape = <u>G O</u> _ _ _ _ _

Not hello = <u>G O</u> _ _ _ _ _

A cart = _ _ <u>G O</u> _

Fairytale lizard = _ _ _ <u>G O</u> _

Didn't remember = _ _ _ <u>G O</u> _

Western state = _ _ _ <u>G O</u> _

Spanish friend = _ _ _ <u>G O</u>

Deep blue = _ _ _ _ <u>G O</u>

City in Illinois = _ _ _ _ _ <u>G O</u>

A Matter of Symmetry

Does your child know what it means to be symmetrical? Explain that this means that his right side and left side are mirror images of each other. He may think the human body is symmetrical because we have two eyes, two arms, and two legs, and they are very much alike. However, ask him to think about whether he uses those sides in the same way.

For example, most people have one hand that they prefer writing with. Ask your child to try writing with a hand he doesn't normally use. Can he do it? (If he can do most things with both hands, that's known as being "ambidextrous.")

VARIATION

Can your child think of all the letters of the alphabet that are symmetrical? Remind him that he should think about "folding" the letters top to bottom, too, not just side to side. (Hint: The letter *Z* is symmetrical horizontally.)

Following the Route

Does your child read the signs and ask questions about the roads you're traveling on? Bring along a road map or atlas and a highlighter. Use a sticker to mark where you're starting and ending your trip. As you travel, have your child highlight each new route or highway as you take it.

Chapter 2

PLANES AND TRAINS

It doesn't matter if your kids get a little excited and loud when you're traveling in your own vehicle. On the other hand, when you're traveling by plane or train you risk bothering other travelers. It's better to have some lower-key activities to keep your kids busy. From artistry to botany and all things in between, here are some ways to keep your little travelers exploring and entertained.

MOUNTAIN WORD SEARCH

If you're traveling through the mountains on a train and need something to entertain your child, just pass her this puzzle and let her surroundings inspire her. In this word grid, see if your child can find thirteen things she might spot on the trip. The words can go backward, forward, up, down, and diagonally.

DEER	**MOOSE**	**SNOW**
EAGLE	**PINECONE**	**TRAIL**
FIREWOOD	**PINE TREE**	**WATERFALL**
HIKER	**ROCKS**	
LOG CABIN	**SKI AREA**	

```
E  S  P  I  N  E  T  R  E  E  F
I  L  N  A  E  R  A  I  K  S  I
E  T  G  O  I  S  T  W  W  E  R
N  N  T  A  W  Y  N  A  I  N  E
O  E  T  H  E  O  T  U  S  A  W
C  N  H  I  K  E  R  D  A  N  O
E  D  T  W  R  E  A  E  E  N  O
N  T  Y  F  S  E  I  I  E  G  D
I  H  A  O  T  F  L  E  E  D  T
P  L  O  T  A  L  S  K  C  O  R
L  M  L  O  G  C  A  B  I  N  L
```

Extra puzzle points: After your child has circled all the listed words, have her read the leftover letters from left to right, and top to bottom. She will find a fast fact about Mount Everest, the world's highest mountain!

Foiled!

One low-mess way to keep your child occupied on trips is with a few sheets of tin foil and a bag of pipe cleaners. Your child can mold and bend the foil and pipe cleaners into creative shapes and maybe even make a masterpiece sculpture. If he's having trouble figuring out what to do with the materials, here are a few suggestions.

- ✦ Create alien creatures.
- ✦ Make zoo or farm animals.
- ✦ Design his own jewelry.
- ✦ Make hats, headbands, crowns, or antennae.
- ✦ Build everyday objects (such as a box, bowl, cup, or envelope).
- ✦ Construct words, letters, or numbers.

Even better, when he's done creating masterpieces, he can simply take them apart and use the materials again later!

BRAIN TEASER: WHEN DOES THIS FLIGHT LAND?

Test your child's brain game by asking him the following brain teaser!

If flying to California takes one and one half hours, and flying to Texas takes two, and flying to Hawaii takes twice as long as a trip to both places, how long is your flight to Hawaii?

What's in a Tree?

If you're traveling by train, you may be going through parts of the country (or countries) your child has never seen before. The landscape—even the plants and trees—can be very different from place to place.

Have your child count all the different types of trees she sees out the window while you're moving slowly. (Keep in mind this might not be the best activity for a child who is prone to motion sickness!)

Your child probably won't know what the different types of trees are, but she can still notice the number of different types and how they're grouped. Explain to her that a "forest" with trees that are very evenly spaced is probably a planted or "planned" forest. Those trees may have been planted there to block the wind, make a house more private, or to sell later for lumber.

Sticky Note Monster Puzzles

With just a pen and some sticky notes, your child can have some monstrous fun! All she has to do is find a flat, smooth surface on which to stick the notes. The airplane window or seatback tray is perfect.

Have her set the notes out in three rows and five columns. On the notes in the top row, have your child draw monster faces. The middle row is for bodies, and the bottom row is for legs. Then she can switch the heads, bodies, and legs to make funny-looking, mixed-up monsters.

If there's more than one person drawing, you can trade body parts to make even stranger-looking monsters!

The Wild Ones

As you travel, ask your child to keep track of and count the number of wild animals that he sees—or that he smells. (Eew, skunk!) If you're traveling through quiet and wooded areas, he might see a deer. And trains usually go through less populated areas where there are more wild animals. He'll have to pay attention, though, because animals in the wild are experts at keeping themselves hidden!

TECH IT UP A NOTCH

Stack the States

This geography game will help your child learn information about all fifty states. The app gives your child an opportunity to learn by flashcard or by playing games. He'll learn about capitals, state shapes, abbreviations, location, state nicknames, state flags, and more. As he solves a puzzle correctly, he can "stack" the state in a pile. Once the stack reaches the finish line, he's won! (iOS, Android, Windows)

Animal Sounds

As you travel by train, you and your child may see animals along the way. Have your child watch out for various animals. When she spots one, have her identify it by the sound it makes. For example, if she sees a cow, she'll say "Moo!" This will lead to a giggle-filled train ride that can bring you to a discussion of what noises some animals actually do make. For example, what does a deer sound like? How about a rabbit?

I'm Going on an Airplane . . .

What would you pack if you were going on an airplane? This twist on a classic alphabet game tests not only your child's memory, but also her pretend packing skills. One of you starts the game by saying, "I'm going on an airplane and I'm bringing an apple" (or any other word that starts with *A*).

The next player has to repeat that sentence and add something that starts with the letter *B*. "I'm going on an airplane and I'm bringing an apple and a balloon." The game continues with each player reciting all the items that were already said and then adding a new word that starts with the next letter in the alphabet. When a player can't remember all the items, he is out.

STATE YOUR NAME

Whether you're at the airport waiting for your flight or at the train station waiting to board, you can hand your child this puzzle to help keep him occupied. Have your child start this puzzle by unscrambling the names of the following twelve states. Then, use the "nicknames" to figure out which states will fit into the grid provided. Remind him that not all of the state names will be used! There's A-M-E-R-I-C-A already in the puzzle to help your child!

WEDLAAER

IOLRAFNCAI

FAIRDLO

DINOALERDHS

UTDSOAHTAOK

ZANIROA

MAAABLA

WIAIHA

NOTEVRM

SLAAAK

YCEKKUTN

ICMNIHGA

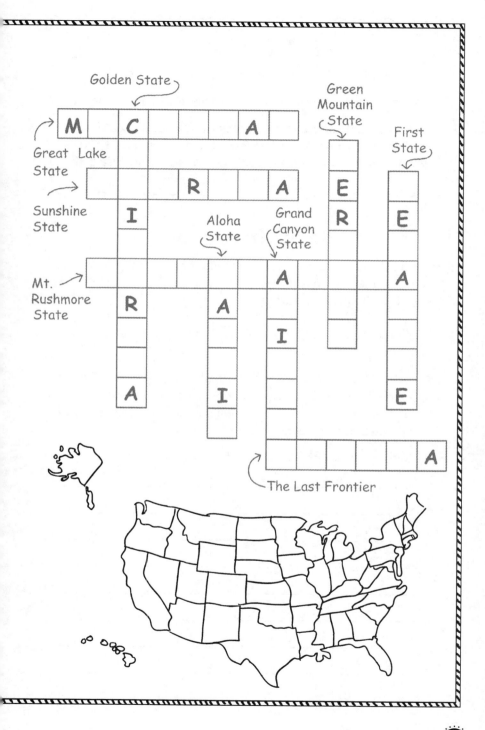

Golden State

M C A

Great Lake State

Green Mountain State

First State

Sunshine State

I R A E E

Aloha State

Grand Canyon State

Mt. Rushmore State

R A A

R A I A

A I E

I A

The Last Frontier

BRAIN TEASER: WHY IS TIME STANDING STILL?

Test your child's brain game by asking him the following brain teaser:

When Juan's plane left the ground it was 2 P.M. After flying for two hours, it landed—but the clocks at the airport showed that it was still 2 P.M. How can this be?

Be an Inventor

Is your child likely to get restless traveling for hours? Challenge him to imagine some ways to make a train or plane more comfortable. Here are a few ideas to get him started.

◆ Fold-down trays for cars so he can write, draw, or eat, the way he does on an airplane.

◆ Little, skinny lamps attached to the back of the seats. Then he can read while his younger siblings sleep, even though it's dark outside. The lamps would also collapse, to keep them out of the way when he's not using them.

◆ Goldfish bowl, with real fish (and a real lid!) to entertain him.

◆ _____

◆ _____

◆ _____

◆ _____

◆ _____

◆ _____

◆ _____

◆ _____

On an Airplane and Feeling Good

If you are on an airplane, your child has the opportunity to be quite an artist. How? By decorating the air sickness bags that come in your seat pocket. If the bag is folded like a brown grocery bag, she can try creating a puppet or two (if she needs to, she can borrow more bags from family members). If you don't have Magic Markers or crayons, a pen or pencil would work just as well.

Keep in mind: Your child has to be feeling well for this activity—otherwise, she might need to grab that bag and use it the way the airline planned!

BRAIN TEASER: HOW CAN THIS BE SO ODD?

Test your child's brain game by asking him the following brain teaser:

When Maddy started school, she was five years old. Now that she is in third grade, she is only six. How can that be? Hint: Maddy's birthday is in February.

How Do You Remember It?

If you've been traveling for a long time, maybe your child has forgotten what your home looks like. Of course, she remembers the big stuff, like the color, and where the garage is, but what about hanging plants, shutters, or a weathervane? Do you have a basketball hoop? A fence or garden? A doghouse or shed?

Depending on where you're going on your trip and who you're visiting, your child may want to show people where she's from or what her favorite room looks like. Is it her bedroom? Have her take a pen, pencil, or crayons and draw her favorite room. Encourage her to think about the little details, like posters she has on the walls, things she keeps on her desk or dresser, or whether she made her bed before you left. When you get home, she can compare her drawing to the real thing—it will be interesting to see what she's remembered.

Watch the Clouds Roll By

Cloud watching is an activity as old as time, but it still stands up. Whether your child is looking at the clouds from an airplane window or from a fast-moving train, he's bound to find some interesting shapes among them. Ask him to tell you what the clouds look like to him. Are there clouds that look like certain animals? Do all the clouds work together to tell a story?

VARIATION

Play cloud I Spy. For example, your child might say, "I spy with my little eye something that looks like a giant teddy bear eating an ice cream cone." Can you find the cloud or clouds he's looking at?

Flight Magazine Fun

Your child's in-flight magazine has more than just the list of snacks you can buy on the fly. It also has a lot of potential to keep her occupied. Give your child a pen or marker and let her circle all the things she'd like to buy if she won a million dollars.

VARIATIONS

Challenge your child to circle all the instances of the words "the" or "is" he finds in the magazine. Ask you child to find something that starts with the letter *A*, then something that begins with *B*. You can have him work his way through the entire alphabet!

BRAIN TEASER: ARE YOU ON THE RIGHT TRACK?

Test your child's brain game by asking him the following brain teaser!

What vehicle travels over the ground at speeds much faster than a car but can also go through mountains?

Egg Carton Mancala

An egg carton makes a perfect portable version of the game Mancala. Add forty-eight beads, beans, or coins, and a couple of sandwich bags, and you're ready to play. The directions are a little complicated to explain and you have to plan this activity in advance, but once you get the gist, the game is easy to play. The object is to collect as many of the objects as you can.

Have your child put four beans in each cup of the egg carton. Put an empty sandwich bag at each end of the egg carton. (One for each player.)

Player One picks up the beans from any cup on his side and, moving clockwise, drops one bean in each of the next egg cups. When he gets to his sandwich bag, he drops one in there, too. He skips Player Two's sandwich bag.

When he runs out of beans, his turn is over *unless* the last bean gets dropped in his sandwich bag. If so, he gets to start again, picking up the beans from any cup he chooses. If not, it's Player Two's turn to choose the beans from any cup and start dropping them.

When a player puts a bead into an empty cup, he gets to take the beans from the cup across from the empty one and put them in his sandwich bag. This means he's taking the beans from his opponent's side of the egg carton.

Keep playing until one player runs out of beans on his side. The player who runs out gets to take all the beans out of the egg carton and put them in his sandwich bag. The player with the most beans wins.

Sticker-ing to It

Stock up on sheets of stickers—most dollar stores sell them, so they're easy to find and inexpensive. If you can locate thematic stickers, that's even better. For example, you might be able to find a sheet of stickers that are all about the airport or one on which the stickers are all steam engines and boxcars.

Give your child a pad of drawing paper, some crayons or markers, and a sheet of stickers. Challenge him to draw a scene that incorporates all of the stickers. For example, if he's using train stickers, he may have to draw the tracks and stations to complete the scene.

TECH IT UP A NOTCH

ScratchJr

This app is perfect for very young programmers. Your child can snap together programming blocks to make stories and games. The blocks will tell his characters how to dance, sing, or move around.

Thanks for the Memories

Having some free time is as good a reason as any for your child to write a letter (or e-mail) of appreciation to a grandparent, teacher, or friend. Of course, she doesn't *have* to have any special reason for writing it, but if she's stuck on a plane or train, for example, or sitting around the terminal, it may be a good time to write a letter thanking her teacher for making school days fun and interesting.

Remind your child to add details to make the letter more personal. She might want to mention a few specific activities or recent lessons that captured her attention. If she hasn't seen her grandparents in a while, she can tell them what she's been doing lately. If she's writing to a friend, she could even try to make plans for the weekend.

Silly Sally

Tell your child there are a few things to know about Silly Sally, such as:

- ✦ She likes jelly, but she doesn't like jam.
- ✦ She likes to be outdoors, but she doesn't like being outside.
- ✦ Silly Sally has good manners, but she's not polite.

Now ask your child to figure out why is Sally so silly. The reason, of course, is because Silly Sally only likes things with double letters. Once your child has figured out the rule, set her loose to see how many Silly Sally statements she can create.

Draw a Caricature

Does your child know what a caricature is? Explain that it's an exaggerated version of something, done in a funny way. Good caricatures usually pick one feature that really stands out, and then make it bigger.

Make sure he understands that caricatures have to be done with caution! He could do a good caricature of someone with big ears, or a big nose, but the person might not like it. If he can, it's better to pick a nice feature and concentrate on that.

It's probably easiest for your child to draw someone who is in the car with him. He might try exaggerating a feature of that face. For example, if he thinks his sister has nice eyes, he can draw a face whose largest feature is the eyes.

He could also make a different kind of caricature. If his brother likes to climb trees and joke around, he might draw a monkey with clown shoes on, climbing up a tree, and then title it something like "Jonathan, in animal form."

ON-THE-GO CHUCKLES

Traveling is a big deal for a kid, and it's even more exciting when she's crossing the state lines on a plane or train. Here your child will find the names of six states. Hand her the book and have her put the names in the correct blanks to make three silly state riddles.

HINT: The pictures will give your child a clue!

NEW JERSEY

TENNESSEE

DELAWARE

MARYLAND

ARKANSAS

IDAHO

What did

_____?

She wore her

_____!

What did

_____?

She saw what

_____!

What did

_____?

She hoed her

_____!

For the Whole Trip

Why not see if your child can keep track of the all miles you travel on this trip? Have him speak with the train conductor, flight attendant, or other transportation official who will be able to tell your child (or find out) how long your trip is.

Give him this easy chart to keep track of the mileage of each leg of the trip. When you're at your destination for the day, he can subtract the beginning number from the end number to get a day's total and record them here:

Miles on Day One: _____

Miles on Day Two: _____

Miles on Day Three: _____

Miles on Day Four: _____

Miles on Day Five: _____

Miles on Day Six: _____

Miles on Day Seven: _____

Miles on Day Eight: _____
(and so on)

When you're done traveling, have your child add up the grand, exhausting total, and put it here:

_____

VARIATION

Before you leave, help him use a program like Google Maps to plan the route of your trip. He can look at all the possible routes and print or save them to his mobile device. Then, at the end of your trip, have your child compare his total to the routes he researched. Did it add up the way he expected?

OMG, WHAT DOES THIS MEAN?

Does your child love social media, texting, and all things electronic? In that case, "MPG" might stand for "multiplayer game" or "most popular girl" instead of "miles per gallon." If that's the case, hand her this book and she should have no problem figuring out what the following acronyms mean!

MYOB

LOL

M_____

Y_____

O_____

B_____

L_____

O_____

L_____

Speak in Song Titles

Everyone loves music, so take this travel time to challenge your child to have a conversation with you using only song titles. For example:

You: "Yesterday" (the Beatles)
Child: "Let It Go" (*Frozen*)
You: "I Knew You Were Trouble" (Taylor Swift)

Since you're both using the songs that you know, it doesn't even matter if you have the same taste in music. As long as the conversation flows, you and your child are doing well!

Create a Jingle

Choose a product—it could be anything from a brand of shoes to toothpaste—and challenge your child to come up with a silly jingle to sell it. He can make up his own tune or use a song he already knows. If he's stuck, give you child a few examples to jump-start his creativity.

Guess the Song

Designate one member of the family to control the MP3 player. Have her choose a song, play the first 30 seconds, and then hit "Pause." Now, the rest of the players have to guess the song. If nobody can guess it, the person with the MP3 player plays another 30 seconds of the song. If it looks like nobody is going to guess the song, your family has to make a choice. You can play it all the way through so everyone can learn a new song or just move on to a more familiar tune.

VARIATION

If you want to mix things up, put your or your child's MP3 player on "Shuffle." When the song begins to play, see who can name it first.

Imaginary Hide-and-Seek

When you're stuck in a plane or a train, there aren't many places for your child to go. However, he can go somewhere in his imagination! Have him imagine a place inside your home to "hide." Since it's only in his imagination, he could even hide in places where he wouldn't fit in real life or in places that aren't usually safe.

The "seeker" has to figure out where the "hider" is hiding by asking questions with yes or no answers. For instance: "Are you hiding somewhere in your bedroom?" See how many questions it takes before your child's hiding place is discovered!

Let's Get Lyrical

Pick a word and see how many songs your child can name that use the word in the title. Once she can't think of any more titles, move on to lyrics or use a variation of the word. Here are some words to get you started.

- ✦ baby
- ✦ blue
- ✦ don't
- ✦ girl
- ✦ happy
- ✦ love
- ✦ run
- ✦ tonight
- ✦ up
- ✦ we

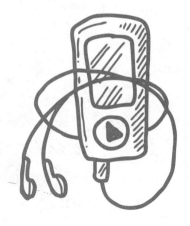

If she gets stuck, you can always give her clues. For instance, you can say, "Remember the lullaby I used to sing you about a cradle in a treetop?"

Activity Books

Your younger child may not be able to read independently, but there are other kinds of books to bring with you to keep to keep her entertained. Here are some to consider.

1. **I Spy.** This series by Jean Marzollo and Walter Wick is masterful at keeping kids entertained. Each two-page picture spread has so many little items carefully hidden to occupy your child for a very long time.
2. **Where's Waldo?** It's surprising how difficult it can be to find one small man wearing a striped shirt and a hat. This series of books will entertain your little sky detective.
3. **Magic Eye.** This series of books is actually a series of optical illusions. Your child will have to look just right to see the 3D image jump off the page. It's worth noting, though, that some people cannot see Magic Eye images. If your child gets frustrated, she may be one of them.

Your older child may be able to read, but that doesn't mean these books won't still entertain him. In fact, you can add new challenges for him. For instance, it may be easy for him to find Waldo, but can he find all the people who look similar and are put in the illustration to make him think he's found Waldo?

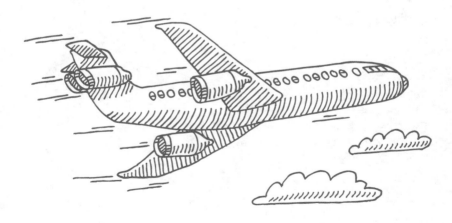

Telephone

This game needs more than two players, so you'll either have to get the whole family to play or make some new friends while you wait at the airport or train terminal! Have the players circle or line up, close enough to whisper in the ear of the person next to them, but not so close that everybody can hear all the players whisper. The first person chooses a sentence or a phrase and whispers it in his neighbor's ear. The neighbor cannot ask for it to be repeated!

He then whispers to his neighbor and so on until you're back at the beginning of the group. The last person to hear the sentence says it out loud. The first person shares what he said in the first place. Do they match?

Front to Back—and Back Again

Has your child ever tried to create a palindrome, a word or phrase that reads the same both forward and backward? "Dad" is a good example. How many palindromes can your child think of? Here are a few to get her started:

- ✦ Madam, I'm Adam
- ✦ A Toyota
- ✦ Dumb mud
- ✦ Never odd or even
- ✦ Wow, mom. Mom, wow!

It can be hard to think of palindromes without seeing them. This game may be a little easier if your child has a piece of paper and a pen to use!

Stare Me Down

Have you ever tried having a stare-down contest with you child? It's fun, it's easy, and it can be amusing to see your child try to keep a straight face. Face your child and challenge him to see which of you can stare into the other person's eyes the longest without blinking or laughing. It's that easy . . . or is it?

GET UP AND GO!

It can be hard to get up in the morning—even when you're out to catch a plane! To help your kids wake up more easily, have them help set the alarm clock the night before. Just don't be like the family seen in the following image!

These family members don't want to miss their shuttle to the airport so everyone sets an alarm clock. Unfortunately, only one clock is set to go off at the correct time. To keep you kids busy when you're figuring out what time you need to head out the door, hand them this book and have them figure out when the family actually needs to get up.

The correct time is halfway between the earliest time and the latest time.

Test Those Reading Skills

Your older child knows how to read, but can she read upside down? Don't worry; she doesn't have to be hanging upside down on a train or plane. She can just flip her book or tablet upside down and see if she can keep reading. Ask her: Is it easy or difficult? Who knows, she may actually be able to read faster upside down than right side up!

Chapter 3
·············

HOTELS AND VACATIONS

It can be a relief when you finally arrive at your vacation destination or hotel. But when you get there, does your child suddenly complain he's bored? From scavenger hunts to complete while you unpack to activities you can do on unexpected rainy days, this chapter has creative ways to quell the complaints.

Follow Simon

This activity is a mashup of the classic games Follow the Leader and Simon Says. It's best played where your child can move freely and not be in other people's way—such as the lobby of your hotel. Your child probably already knows how to mimic the movements of the leader and to follow the directions when Simon says. This game combines those ideas.

Designate one person to be "Simon." Simon chooses a motion for the other players to make, such as waving their right hand. He then says, "Follow Simon in waving your right hand." Since he's also the leader, he's going to make a motion, too.

Here's the catch—as the leader, Simon can choose to make any motion he wants (such as hopping on one foot). It doesn't have to be the same as what Simon *said*. If he had said "Follow Simon," the rest of the players have to do what Simon said. If he just says, "Wave your right hand," the players have to imitate what he's doing, not what he said.

A SHORT TRIP

Most people travel from where they live and work to a vacation spot so they can relax. Can your child get from "TRAVEL" to "RELAX" in just four steps? In each step he can do only one of three things: omit a letter, switch two letters with each other, or change one letter into another letter. Hand him the book and have him write his changes, step by step, on the lines provided.

TRAVEL

1. _____

2. _____

3. _____

4. RELAX

Alphabetical Barn: Animals from A to Z

If you're visiting the zoo or a farm on your vacation, bring a small pad of paper with you so your child can write down the names of all the animals she encounters. At the end of the day, have your child alphabetize the list. Did she find animals from A to Z?

TECH IT UP A NOTCH

Evernote

Let your child use this note-taking app on your mobile device to "write down" the animals—it's one less pad of paper to keep track of! He can also take a picture of each animal to help him remember what unusual animals—like emus or platypuses—look like. (iOS, Android, Windows)

Be a Plant Scientist

As you vacation in various parts of the country, your child will probably notice some nice flowers, weird rocks, odd shells, colored leaves, and more. Find a box or bag to collect some of the more interesting objects she finds. She can label each "natural treasure" by taping a little note to it. The note might say, "This is an elm leaf" or "granite rock." (She might need to figure that out for sure when you get home.) On the other hand, the note might just say where she found it ("Florida campsite near Orlando," for example) and on what date. That will help her identify it better when you get home—and it will make a nice souvenir.

Telling Stories 'Round the Campfire

Campfire stories are a great activity for camping vacations, but you don't have to actually sit around a fire to tell them. If you're in a hotel, put blankets on the floor to make it feel more like a camp or just curl up in your beds and tell "hotel stories."

Go around the "campfire" and have each person tell a story. The taller the tale, the better! If your child is having trouble getting started, tell the story of Paul Bunyan and Babe the Blue Ox or make up your own ridiculous story. Your child is bound to be amused to hear you tell what sounds like out-and-out lies.

VARIATIONS

Tell stories about your most embarrassing moments, your first memories, or take turns telling a story about something you did together. You might be surprised to hear how differently you and your child viewed the event!

LET'S GET PACKING

It may look to your child as if it's easy to get packed and planned for the vacation activity of the day, but you know it's not. While you're getting organized for the day, keep your child busy and give her a better sense of how much there is to do! Hand her this book and a pencil so she can learn more about vacation planning.

In the space next to the word box (or on a separate piece of paper) have your child list all the words in the boxes with the number one. Then have her do the same for the words in the boxes numbered two, three, four, five, and six. She'll have to unscramble the words that go with each number to create a sentence. In the end she'll have six sentences that explain what it took to get ready for a hiking trip.

1. _____

2. _____

3. _____

4. _____

5. _____

6. _____

1 Call	4 and	2 bug	1 to	5 extra	2 block
4 bottles,	1 Kelly	5 and	3 flashlight	6 Find	4 snacks,
2 Buy	5 Pack	6 bird	4 water	7 directions	2 spray.
3 the	4 Fill	1 for	6 and	5 ponchos	6 books.
1 Short	6 binoculars	3 Check	2 sun	3 batteries.	2 and
4 chocolate!	1 park.	4 make	5 socks.	1 State	4 get

Puddle Play

There's nothing like going on a trip and waking up to rain and drizzle. But, if you're willing to deal with some wet shoes and socks, that rain doesn't have to ruin your vacation. Many young kids love puddles, but don't often get a chance to stomp in and explore them, so take a vacation from the rules and let your child be a puddle splasher!

Ask the front desk for extra plastic cups, coffee stirrers, coffee filters, and other small essentials. Your child can use them to make a boat for the bigger puddles. He can also experiment to see what floats and what sinks, as well as which things absorb water and which repel it.

Memory!

How many different things were for sale in the last vending machine your child looked at? It could have been a soda vending machine at the hotel, or a snack dispenser at an amusement park. What about the beverage choices at the hotel's breakfast buffet? Does your child remember the choices that were available?

City Rhymes

In this rhyming game, have your family come up with a word or phrase that rhymes with the city you're in or are nearest to. For example, if you're near Minneapolis, you might say Indianapolis. An easier city might be New York, which rhymes with silly phrases like "blue fork." When the family runs out of rhymes for the current location, it's time to start thinking of rhymes for the next stop on your trip!

Furniture Dance

In this activity, family members come up with names of pieces of furniture that you'd find in a hotel. Some examples are "desk," "bed," and "chair." As you go, you'll get to harder ones like "ottoman" and "rollaway bed." When thinking of hotel room furniture gets harder to do, remind your child of other places in the hotel, like the pool or the lobby. Keep playing until nobody can think of another piece of furniture.

BRAIN TEASER: SOLVE THIS MINI MOTEL MYSTERY

Test your child's brain game by asking him the following brain teaser:

When Mini's family pulled up at the motel, Mini, her parents, and twelve brothers and sisters poured out of the car. How could that happen?

The Postcard No One Has Ever Seen

Buy a blank postcard or let your child use a piece of cardboard to draw her own. Ask her to think about the scenery she's seen throughout your trip to get some inspiration for her drawing.

If she wants to make her postcard look more professional, she can try drawing with a realistic sense of perspective. First, she can draw the things in the foreground. Those should go toward the bottom of the postcard. (Since they're nearest to her, they're probably covering up the things that are farther away.)

Then suggest she draw some things in the middle. Lastly, she might want to add the farthest away things at the top of the postcard. What should she put in? It doesn't matter—anything she wants! Even if it's a big monster, three suns, or a dozen moons shining over Walt Disney World.

WEATHER DIARY

A more involved activity for your child while you're at a hotel is to keep track of the temperature and other weather details during your trip. He can do this for every day of the vacation or for just a few days. The more the weather varies, the more interesting this activity will be (but 98°F might make him feel too hot to be all that interested).

Have him try to "take the day's temperature" at about the same time every day. Noon might be a good time, or you can do it when you leave the hotel for your day's adventures. If you have a car with a thermometer, have your child use that to determine the temperature. If you don't, your child can check a weather app on your phone, or the hotel lobby may also have a computer screen or posting of the day's weather. He can use Fahrenheit or Celsius—or go all out and record both! Here's a sample chart he can fill out:

Today is _____ (the date)

Temperature: _____°F or _____°C

It was (check one)

☐ sunny

☐ mostly sunny

☐ cloudy

☐ raining

☐ snowing

☐ sleeting

☐ stormy

Today is _____ (the date)

Temperature: _____°F or _____°C

It was (check one)

☐ sunny   ☐ snowing

☐ mostly sunny   ☐ sleeting

☐ cloudy   ☐ stormy

☐ raining

Today is _____ (the date)

Temperature: _____°F or _____°C

It was (check one)

☐ sunny   ☐ snowing

☐ mostly sunny   ☐ sleeting

☐ cloudy   ☐ stormy

☐ raining

Today is _____ (the date)

Temperature: _____°F or _____°C

It was (check one)

☐ sunny   ☐ snowing

☐ mostly sunny   ☐ sleeting

☐ cloudy   ☐ stormy

☐ raining

HEADING HOME

You have finished your vacation at the beach—now it's time to return home. Hand your child the book and a pencil so he can make the journey on paper. Ask him to start at the word SEA. Then he has to travel one space at a time making compound words as he goes until reaching the word HOME. Your child can move up and down, and side to side, but not diagonally!

START SEA	SHELL	FISH	HOOK
HORSE	BACK	HAND	BALL
FLY	YARD	OUT	GAME
PAPER	STICK	BREAK	DOWN
BACK	FIRE	FAST	TOWN FINISH

Let's Take a Long Walk

Suggest to your child that he draw a picture of himself walking and carrying all of his luggage. Then have him figure out how long it would take to walk the distance of your trip. For example, if your trip has already been 500 miles and he could only walk two and a half miles per hour (that's a long way to lug a lot of luggage), it would take him about 200 hours.

Does your child think he could walk for fourteen hours a day? That would leave him nine hours per day to sleep, and one hour for either eating or resting. And even then, it would take him at least fourteen days to get as far as you are now!

Web Detective

If your family has time, take half an hour to browse the website of the city you're visiting. Your child can visit the hotel computer (usually at the business center) before bedtime or use his smartphone before you head out for the day.

What new things can your child learn about the city? Look for things like upcoming events, recommended tourist sites, and city news. Walking tours and parks are a great way to see a city and watch the people, too. Once your child has had a chance to learn more, ask him to fill you in on his research. It might be fun to visit one of the places he recommends!

TECH IT UP A NOTCH

My Little Suitcase

This app is a great way to keep your child occupied as you plan a vacation or while you're on your way to one. Your child can choose the type of vacation he wants to go on, grab items from the menu, and fill his suitcase. Once he's packed and ready to "go," your child will be able to play vacation-themed games. (iOS)

Restaurant Investigations

If you go to a local restaurant while you're on vacation—one that is run by people from that town, serves what people in that town like, and attracts those townspeople—your child can be a "road detective."

If your server isn't too busy and you're okay with your child making conversation with strangers, she can ask some questions to learn more about the place you're visiting. Usually people like talking about themselves and things they know about. If your child starts a polite conversation, and is genuinely interested in discovering some things, most people will be happy to talk to her. Your road detective can ask questions like:

- ◆ Do you live in this town?
- ◆ What do you like best about it?
- ◆ What do people do on the weekends for fun?
- ◆ What is the most popular dish on the menu?
- ◆ What's your favorite item on the menu?
- ◆ What makes your town different from other places?

As you begin this activity, feel free to remind your child that it's not polite to interrupt people who are eating or a server who is very busy.

BRAIN TEASER: CAN YOU NAME THE WORLD TRAVELER?

Test your child's brain game by asking him the following brain teaser:

What can travel all over the world, without anyone seeing it?

A Story about Five Things

If you're stuck in your hotel room on a rainy day and running out of ideas to entertain your child, try a "five things story." Choose any five things to place on a table or bed. For example, a small toy truck, a hairbrush, a bottle of hotel shampoo, a room key, and a sock. Then, challenge your child and the rest of the family to tell any story that includes those five items. A collection of random items for which there isn't an obvious connection is likely to prompt a more interesting story.

For more object ideas, look at the list that follows . . . that will keep everyone busy!

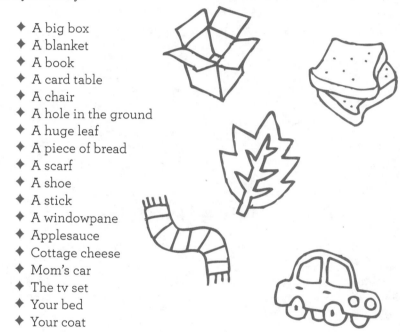

- ✦ A big box
- ✦ A blanket
- ✦ A book
- ✦ A card table
- ✦ A chair
- ✦ A hole in the ground
- ✦ A huge leaf
- ✦ A piece of bread
- ✦ A scarf
- ✦ A shoe
- ✦ A stick
- ✦ A windowpane
- ✦ Applesauce
- ✦ Cottage cheese
- ✦ Mom's car
- ✦ The tv set
- ✦ Your bed
- ✦ Your coat

For older children, you may want to try this with some objects that aren't physically there (the North Pole, a lion, a spoon, a shooting star, and the sun, for example).

Make Up a Song

Is your child one of those kids who can make up a song about anything? Why not encourage her to make up her own song about where you are? Ask her to think about what makes this vacation unique—she can even make a list of some of the things she has seen, the places you've been, or the names of the attractions nearby.

She can also list some of the funny names of the towns or add in some of the more classic and funny things other family members have said on this part of your trip.

Once your child has a list of topics, she can decide if she wants to make up the music or use the tune of a song she already knows. Once your child has her act all set, let her perform it for you!

Ninety-Nine Bottles of . . .

Everybody knows this song and its tune! Even though as you get down to about seventy-five bottles the average parent wants to scream, it can be a great way to pass the time when you're in traffic or waiting for the whole family to get ready to leave for the day's adventures.

Encourage your child to be creative to keep the game interesting for everyone. Every time he goes down one number (such as ninety-nine, ninety-eight, ninety-seven, and so on), he has to think of a different beverage or liquid. For example, start with ninety-nine bottles of milk, then ninety-eight bottles of soda, on down to twenty bottles of shampoo on the wall. If he gets stuck, take turns thinking of a new item, until everyone runs out of ideas. Then, feel free to tell him that he *has to stop singing that song!*

HOTEL
SCAVENGER HUNT

Looking for a way to occupy your child while you get settled and unpacked at your hotel? Send her on a hotel scavenger hunt! Here are some lists of items for her to find, questions for her to answer, and things to take pictures of.

TO FIND:

☐ Local map
☐ Do Not Disturb sign
☐ Brochure for a local tourist attraction
☐ Takeout menu for a restaurant
☐ Envelope
☐ Pad of paper with the hotel logo on it
☐ Coffee stirrer
☐ Tea bag or coffee
☐ A vending machine item that doesn't have chocolate in it
☐ Business card

QUESTIONS TO ANSWER:

☐ How many pillows are in your room?
☐ By what time must you check out of the hotel?
☐ Is there a fitness room in the hotel?
☐ What machines are in the fitness room?
☐ What is the name of the attendant working at the desk?
☐ How many floors does the hotel have?
☐ How old do you have to be to go to the pool without an adult?

TO TAKE PICTURES OF:

☐ An employee's nametag
☐ EXIT sign
☐ Something on the room service menu for less than $10
☐ An In Case of Emergency plan diagram
☐ A room number in which all the numbers are the same

Since she's already explored the hotel, she can lead you to the pool for some rest and relaxation when you're finally unpacked!

TECH IT UP A NOTCH

StoryLines

This app combines word play and drawing. It's sort of a high-tech version of the old game Telephone. The first player receives a common phrase that he then has to illustrate on the screen (using his finger). Then he passes the device to the next player who has to give the drawing a title—without knowing the phrase. The next player illustrates that title and the game continues. (iOS)

Who's That Guy and What's His Story?

Is your child a people watcher? Put that habit to good use by asking him to make up stories about the people he's watching. Give him a pad of paper and something to write with so he can write down his stories. (It's better than telling them out loud—kids aren't always great about talking quietly.)

If your child isn't sure how to get started, ask him to start with the question, "Why?" For example, "Why is this person here? Why did he come here today? Why is he by himself?"

BRAIN TEASER: THE ROLLER COASTER RIDE

Test your child's brain game by asking him the following brain teaser:

If it takes 12 minutes for the Gowen family to wait for a ride on the roller coaster, and 5 minutes for everyone to get off it, how many minutes are spent screaming?

Start Jumping on the Bed!

Let your child do all the things you tell him he can't do at home. That's right, you're not washing the sheets, so let him build a fort! Play trash-can basketball with a rolled-up pair of socks. Turn on the TV and let him watch a kid-friendly channel you don't get at home. It's not your bed, so why can't he jump on it? Just try to pick your time thoughtfully—jumping on the bed at six in the morning might make your downstairs neighbors a little grouchy!

Up Close and Personal

If your child likes to draw, put her to work drawing what she sees from where she's sitting. It's a great way to practice perspective. When she draws a room from within the room, she can draw the ceiling as sloping upward, toward the upper corners of the page. It's almost as if she's looking down a narrow tunnel, or as though she's playing one of those first-person perspective video games, where the tunnels scroll around and over her as she walks down them. Your child may find this activity difficult, but fun.

 Check Out Local Wildlife

If your family is going camping, hiking, or fishing, many areas have websites that tell you more about where you will be visiting. Many have sections for kids to play games, become acquainted with the kind of wildlife they might see, and offer tips for how to have safe fun outdoors! For an example of the kind of information your child might find, visit the New Hampshire Fish and Game website: *www.wildnh.com/Kids/ kids.htm.*

Pretend Fred

If your child isn't much for drawing, but enjoys storytelling, this is a great activity for him. Have him make up a story about an outrageous, fictitious character that lives in your city or a place he would like to visit. For inspiration, remind your child of the myths or fairly tales he may have read with you or in school.

For example, if you're in rural Kansas, he could write about "Tornado Tom." He might say that, "Tornado Tom is a young boy who—without wanting to—makes tornadoes appear wherever he goes. When Tom lived in Chicago, he found that the tornadoes were wrecking his city. So he moved to Kansas, where everything was spread out. Now, the tornadoes don't cause as much damage, because there's not as much stuff around for them to destroy."

BRAIN TEASER: HOW DID THE PLANE LAND?

Test your child's brain game by asking him the following brain teaser:

When the storm hit and the plane attempted to land, everyone in the air and on the ground was speechless. Yet somehow they communicated the directions to land. How?

Digital Picture Puzzles

Put those pics on your mobile device to work entertaining your child! Download a puzzle-making app like Puzzle Maker for Kids (*http://scottadelman.com/puzzle-maker-for-kids-create-your-own-jigsaw-puzzles-from-pictures/*) to turn photos into digital jigsaw puzzles. You also can make a low-tech version of this activity—just print a picture from a previous vacation on heavyweight paper, cut it into unusual shapes, and pop it into an envelope for your child. Your child will love to make a puzzle out of a family photo. As she puts it together, she can try to guess what the photo is and where it was taken!

FAMILY ALBUM

Aaron and Jason both wanted to take a picture of their parents at the scenic rest area. But somehow each picture turned out a little different! Hand your child this book and ask her if she can find the eight differences between the two snapshots?

What's Happening Locally?

Part of the fun of going somewhere new for vacation is finding out how your destination differs from home. Encourage your child to ask the front desk for a copy of the local newspaper. You may need to explain that some smaller towns have newspapers that only come out weekly, but that most places have "dailies." If you find a weekly, can he tell how it's different from a daily? (Hint: It probably won't be a thick paper.)

Ask him to compare the news from your vacation spot to the news at home. Are there similarities? Differences? Does he think any of the stories are being reported at home, too?

VARIATION

Try to find a local radio station to listen to in the car or a local news station to watch. Ask: Can he tell how big the city is by the kind of news they report? What kinds of problems do they report? Are there more human-interest stories than crime stories? What does that tell him about where you are?

Castaways!

If your child was about to be stranded on an island, what would he do? That's the premise of this game! Ask your child what items would he pack with him or take from the ship that is sinking. Can he defend his choice to take those items with him? What if he could only bring one thing—what would it be?

Once everybody in your family has had a turn to answer these questions, it's time to figure out how all of your items combined can be used to help you get home. Can you use the strings from Dad's guitar to lash together trees and make a raft? Can the pages of your son's books be burned for heat using the matches his sister brought with her?

Remember, the items you all choose don't have to make sense. In fact, the sillier they are, the funnier your escape scenarios are likely to be!

WHAT ARE YOU DOING ON VACATION?

Your child may have already calculated how many miles per gallon you're getting on this trip, so he knows what MPG stands for, but can he figure out what these acronyms mean? Here are a couple of vacation-related hints to help him out.

1. If you visit New England in the fall, you might do this after taking a hayride in the apple orchard.

P _____

Y _____

O _____

"I can do this all by myself!"

PYO

2. If you visit Nevada and are a believer in the supernatural, you may go to Area 51 to look for evidence that one of these landed on earth.

U _____

F _____

O _____

What is it?

I don't know, but it's moving fast!

UFO

Treasured Moments

If your child were to find a treasure chest, what would she hope to find inside? Encourage her to draw a picture of the treasure chest. She can also write a story of how she found it, what is inside, and what she plans to do with the treasure.

She may also want to create a vacation treasure chest, too. Ask the clerk at the hotel desk for a small empty box (housekeeping is likely to have one). Your child can decorate the box with crayons or markers and use it to collect "treasures" from your vacation. Don't look inside, though! Let it be her secret. When you get home from vacation, she can unpack it and show you what she "treasured" the most on your trip.

BRAIN TEASER:
IS THIS A THREE-RING CIRCUS?

Test your child's brain game by asking him the following brain teaser:

When the circus came to town, everyone was surprised—even the lion tamer, as he discovered 7 new lion cubs in the lion cage. Before long, everyone agreed it would be best to separate the feisty cubs. But how? Then the ringmaster had an idea: "I know a way you can place 3 large rings to make 7 sections, one for each cub." Do you know how to do that?

State the States

Can you and your child name all fifty states? Test his knowledge of the United States by seeing how many states he can name without referring to a map. It may be hard to keep track of what he's already named, so he may want to write them down as he says them. It may help to try to name them in alphabetical order. Here are some hints to help:

✦ Four states start with the letter *A* (Alabama, Alaska, Arizona, and Arkansas)

✦ Three states start with the letter *C* (California, Colorado, and Connecticut)

✦ One state starts with the letter *D* (Delaware)

✦ One state starts with the letter *F* (Florida)

✦ One state starts with the letter *G* (Georgia)

✦ One state starts with the letter *H* (Hawaii)

✦ Four states start with the letter *I* (Idaho, Illinois, Indiana, and Iowa)

✦ Two states start with the letter *K* (Kansas and Kentucky)

✦ Eight states start with the letter *M* (Maine, Maryland, Massachusetts, Michigan, Minnesota, Mississippi, Missouri, and Montana)

✦ Eight states start with the letter *N* (Nebraska, Nevada, New Hampshire, New Jersey, New Mexico, New York, North Carolina, and North Dakota)

✦ Three states start with the letter *O* (Ohio, Oklahoma, and Oregon)

✦ One state starts with the letter *P* (Pennsylvania)

✦ One state starts with the letter *R* (Rhode Island)

✦ Two states start with the letter *S* (South Carolina and South Dakota)

✦ Two states start with the letter *T* (Tennessee and Texas)

✦ One state starts with the letter *U* (Utah)

✦ Two states start with the letter *V* (Vermont and Virginia)

✦ Four states start with the letter *W* (Washington, West Virginia, Wisconsin, and Wyoming)

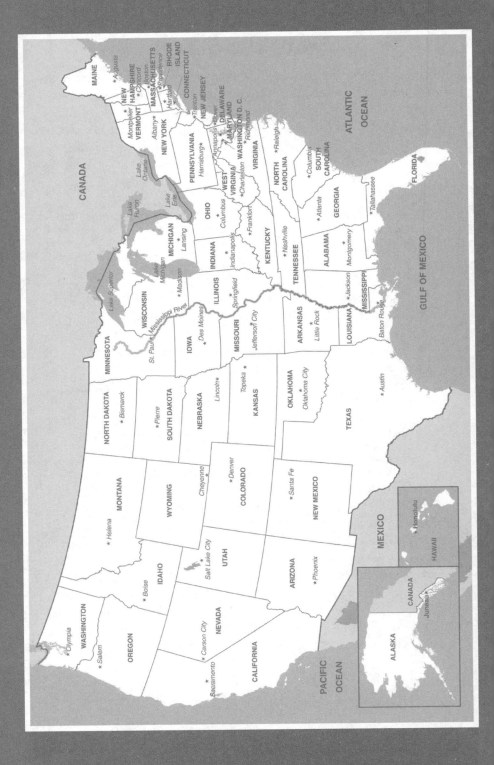

Across the Nation

What can your child do with a map of the United States? Pass this book over to her along with a box of crayons or markers! Here's a list of things she can do to keep herself occupied and learning as you travel by train or plane.

- ✦ Have your child study the capitals of each state. Take the book back from your child and quiz her on the state capitals.
- ✦ Color all the states she's visited yellow.
- ✦ Color all the states you're traveling to on this trip blue.
- ✦ Color all the states she wants to go to red.
- ✦ Use a pen to write in all the state nicknames that she knows. For example, Texas is known as the Lone Star State and Maine is called the Pine Tree State and is also known as Vacationland.
- ✦ Have her draw a small picture on each state of something she knows about it or that it is known for. For example, she may want to draw Mickey Mouse ears on Florida or a peach on Georgia.
- ✦ Map the route from where you live to where you're going. How many states will you pass through? Is there more than one way to get there?
- ✦ Identify how many states aren't bordered by another state. How many are bordered by one other state? Two? Three or more?

I'm Going to . . .

For this game, you'll need a map, atlas, or a map app on your mobile device. Open the map or pull up a small area on the map app. Find a town, road name, or other landmark on the map. Tell your child what it is and then hand the map to him. He now has five minutes to find that place on the map!

AT THE ZOO

If you're going to be spending a vacation day at the zoo, have your child do this puzzle while you're waiting in line to get in: Hand her the book and have her find the ten ways the following scenes differ from one another. Then, once she finds the differences, have her tell you what in the pictures she's most excited to see as you tour the zoo.

Fast-Food Finds

Assign each member of your family a fast-food restaurant that you're likely to see throughout your vacation. Some to consider include Burger King, Wendy's, Pizza Hut, Sonic, and McDonald's. Every time somebody sees "their" restaurant on a billboard or road sign, they earn a point. Each time they spot the actual building or see an ad on TV, they earn two points.

Keep track of the points in a small notepad or on a note app on your mobile device. By the end of the trip, you all might be surprised by how many fast-food restaurants you've all seen!

Hangman

Hangman is a pretty classic game and it's perfect to play in the hotel room with your child as you're waiting to start your day. Grab the complimentary pad of paper and pen from the desk and have your child draw dashes to represent the letters of the word or phrase she's thinking of. She should also draw the Hangman frame. As you try to guess the word, one letter at a time, she needs to either fill in the correct blanks or draw a body part on the frame. If you guess before the whole person is drawn, you win. Otherwise, it's time to start over!

Capture the Box

The object of this pen and paper game is for a player to connect dots to make as many boxes as possible.

1. Draw an 8 × 8 grid of dots like this:

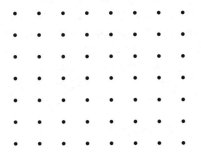

2. Take turns drawing a line between dots. You can draw a vertical or horizontal line, but not a diagonal. You may want to use two different color markers to know which line belongs to which player.
3. Once a player draws the line that completes a square, he "claims" the box by putting his initials in it. He then gets another turn.

When the grid is complete, the player with his initials in the most boxes wins.

Shhh

Kill some time at the hotel in the morning by playing Shhh! This game starts with one person choosing a common word (such as "and," "the," or "because") to be the banned word. After he tells the other players the banned word, that person then has to ask questions of all the other players—and none of them can use the banned word in their sentences!

Of course, the player asking questions should try to make the others say the banned word. For instance, if the word is "because," he may want to ask questions that begin with the phrase, "Why did you . . . ?" When a player uses the banned word, everybody gets to say, "SHHH!"

Cobbler, Cobbler

Best for younger children, this activity is easily played in your hotel room when you're waiting for the rest of the family to be ready to head out for the day. Have your child lie on his back so you can play with his feet. Then chant the following words and use the corresponding motions:

Cobbler, cobbler, mend my shoe
(wiggle his feet to and fro)
Have it done by half past two
Stitch it up and stick it down
(tap lightly around the edges of his feet)
Now nail the heel all around
(hammer his heel gently with your fist)

Younger kids will love the physical contact, and this may just hold you over long enough to get everyone on their way out the door.

Drumstick

On your way out of the hotel, grab a plastic spoon, coffee mixer, or paper cup, then take your child outside and encourage him to tap on different things to hear the different sounds they make. Talk about what she hears. The items your child can tap on are endless, but can include:

- ✦ Bricks
- ✦ A tree trunk
- ✦ A metal pole
- ✦ A rain gutter

This is a great way to keep your child entertained while you're waiting for a bus or a taxi to take you sightseeing!

Shine a Flashlight

If your child is antsy before heading out to dinner or before hopping into bed, this game will keep him occupied. Simply take a flashlight—or use the one in your phone—and shine the flashlight on your child's body parts (hair, feet, hands, etc.) or onto objects in the room and ask your child to name them. It's a good activity for younger kids and it's sure to have your kid turning off the lights faster than you ever thought possible.

Birds That Fly

This follow-the-leader activity is perfect when your child needs to get the wiggles out after a long day of sightseeing! Simply call out an animal and an action for your child to imitate. For example, when you call out "Birds fly!" your child should flap his arms like a bird. There are many possible directives, such as frogs that hop, snakes that slither, or horses that gallop. Try to fool your child once in a while by calling out a silly directive. For example, say, "Fish hop!" Then, if you fail to trick him, he gets a chance to be the caller.

Buzzing Bee

Best for younger kids, this activity is perfect if you're sitting on the beach or are tired after a long day of sightseeing on vacation. Here, your child is the bee and you are the flower. Since you're the flower, you sit or stand in one place. Your child is the bee who can buzz all around you and then return for pollen. This allows your child to burn off that extra energy while giving you the chance to relax!

VARIATION

There are many possible variations for this activity! For example, you can be the moon and your child can be a spaceship. Or perhaps you are a gas station and your child is the car. Be inventive and try to tie this activity back to your vacation!

CAVE CODE

If you're vacationing in a place where you'll be touring some caves, this activity will get your child excited about sightseeing! Legends tell of caves filled with pirate treasure or archaeological finds and, if your child can break the secret code found there, she can find the hidden treasure. Hand her the book and have her follow the instructions to see which square to push to enter the ancient cave. But she needs to be careful! If she pushes the wrong one, the cave could fall in!

Here are her clues:

The key is in the row with a hand next to it.

The key has a sun above or below it.

Going in a straight line, the key is three squares away from a bird.

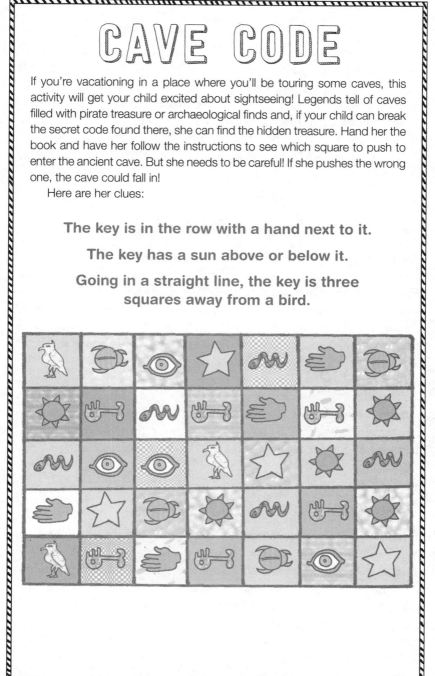

Beach Obstacle Course

If you're vacationing at the beach, all you need is a shovel and a stick to keep your child entertained while you sit back and read a magazine. If you have a younger child, draw a winding line in the sand around your chair or towel to create a path for him to follow. Then, use the shovel to create ditches and gullies along the path for your child to jump over. You can also build up mounds for him to climb over or walk around.

If your child is older, have him create this obstacle course on his own and just sit back and relax!

Sunny Bedtime

If you're vacationing in a sunny locale, this activity will let you help your kids think about what would happen if there were too much sun. Ask your child what it would be like to have bright sunshine outside when she's getting ready for bed. Would she have trouble sleeping? If so, what would she need to block out the sun's rays to get a good night's sleep? Blackout curtains? A sleep mask? A hand over her face?

VARIATION

Instead of too much sun, have your child think about what would happen if it were dark all the time. What would it be like to wake up in complete darkness? To have to go to school in the dark? To go to the beach in the dark? How would total darkness affect your vacation?

Noisy Ice

If you're in the hotel restaurant or lobby and need a way to entertain your child until breakfast comes or you head out for the day, all you need is a glass of warm water from the beverage station and some ice cubes. Drop the ice cubes into the glass of warm water and have your child listen to how they crack and pop. Explain to him that glaciers and icebergs make the same types of noises when the ice breaks off and falls into the ocean—which can be especially fun to discuss if you're on a cruise! Then let him grab another cup of ice and give it a try on his own!

LOOP THE ZOO

If you're visiting the zoo while on vacation, ask your child "What goes black, white, black, white, black, white?" Pass this book to your child with a box of crayons or markers and she'll be on the route to finding out! All she has to do is follow the path through the zoo to take Zack to three of his favorite animals. Along the way, she can collect the letters that spell out three different answers to the riddle.

Why Are You Tickling Yourself?

Is your child ticklish? If so, it's possible that amid all the laughter he hasn't noticed that it's almost impossible to tickle yourself. If he doesn't believe you, ask him to try it by tickling the palm of his hand. When he doesn't laugh, you try tickling his hand. Point out it's the element of surprise that makes all the difference.

If he's disappointed, here are a few ways he can try to "surprise" himself enough to get a little giggle.

- ✦ Challenge him to try to tickle the roof of his mouth with his tongue. When he moves his tongue lightly on his palate, it may cause a tickly feeling.
- ✦ Have him run a hairbrush lightly in the very ticklish spots on the bottom of his foot, in the crook of his elbow, or behind his knee. If that doesn't do it, a softer item with a lighter touch might work. Let him experiment with feathers, pipe cleaners, and craft pom-poms!
- ✦ Ask your child to close his eyes. Then, have him move his fingertips lightly in a circle on his bare arm or leg. If he's not able to see his fingers touching his skin, he might actually trick himself into being ticklish!

BRAIN TEASER: WHICH DOESN'T BELONG?

Test your child's brain game by asking her the following brain teaser:

Which one of these does not belong to the set?
Lion, tiger, elephant, and polar bear.

WHERE IN THE WORLD?

Does your child know some of the most popular vacation spots in the world? Maybe you're even visiting one of them right now! Pass this book to her so she can find out. All she has to do is unscramble the names of eight different places around the world. Then she can match each one to a riddle to discover those eight popular vacation spots.

1. Where do fish go on vacation?

2. Where do songbirds go on vacation?

3. Where do zombies go on vacation?

4. Where do Thanksgiving birds go on vacation?

5. Where do geometry teachers go on vacation?

6. Where do locksmiths go on vacation?

nliFnad   hTe ranCay nsIlsad

eruTky   ehT edaD aSe

auCb   heT arlFoid seKy

Chapter 4

....

THINGS TO DO WHEN YOU'RE WAITING AROUND

What do waiting rooms, waiting in line, and waiting for a table in a restaurant have in common? It's more than just the word "wait." Waiting rooms and lines require kids to be patient in front of other people. If patience isn't your child's strong suit to begin with, it can make for a very long and uncomfortable wait. If you don't have a bag of tricks to pull activities out of, don't worry. This chapter is full of fun and entertaining activities that will keep your kids occupied no matter where you're waiting.

Snort, Cough, and Sneeze

It's no fun being in the waiting room of the doctor's office, even when your child is there for a well-child checkup. There are bound to be sick kids there, too. Pass the time by having your child count the number of times other people sneeze, cough, snort, and sniffle while she waits for her turn. Just remind her to count discreetly. Yelling "Are they gross or what?" is bound to take the fun out of the game very quickly!

TECH IT UP A NOTCH

Caillou Check Up!

This app uses a popular PBS Kids' character to help your child learn more about what a visit to the doctor entails. Your child can check Caillou's vision, height, weight, and vital signs. She can also play games to learn more about the body and the tools a doctor uses. (iOS, Android)

What If We Looked Different?

If your child is struggling to stay patient while she waits, pique her interest by imagining what would happen in some unusual situations. Here are some interesting conversation starters to keep your child occupied while you wait. What would we do if . . .

> . . . we had pincers for hands like lobsters?
> . . . we all knew how to fly?
> . . . we had inline skates or scooters instead of feet?
> . . . we had webbed hands like ducks?
> . . . we could only talk in sneezes?
> . . . we had antennae?
> . . . people were all nocturnal, like owls?
> . . . we had four eyes (two on the back of our heads)?

What other strange possibilities can she think of?

Clapping Categories

It's time to put those knees to use! Begin a quiet tap/clap rhythm by tapping your knees and clapping your hands. Make it simple because you and your child will have to keep it up for the whole game. For instance, try tapping your knees twice and then clapping twice.

Once you all have the rhythm going, ask your child to choose a category. Colors, numbers, animals, or foods are easy ones to start with. Each player has to think of a word that fits that category. As you go back and forth, you have to say your word in time with the rhythm.

For example:

tap, tap, clap, clap, "Green!"
tap, tap, clap, clap, "Red!"
tap, tap, clap, clap, "Yellow!"

When someone makes a mistake, by either missing the beat or saying something that's not part of the category, he's out.

BRAIN TEASER:
HOW MANY PEOPLE CAME FOR PIZZA?

Test your child's brain game by asking him the following brain teaser!

When Sara invited some friends over to watch a movie, her parents decided to order pizza for all of them. When the delivery came, there were 2 large pizzas and 1 small one. If a large pizza serves 8 people and a small pizza serves 4, how many friends were at Sara's house?

Famous Initials

In this game, each person has to come up with the name of a famous person whose last name starts with a certain letter. As a group, you can decide whether the people need to be real people, or if famous names of fictional people count, too. For example, if you are trying to come up with famous people whose last names begin with "P," you'd say "Katy Perry," and the next person might say "Harry Potter."

To mix the game up a little, you can also say a set of initials, tell your child if the person is real or fictional, and then have her guess who it is. Give clues as needed, like "This person sings a song that's named after the sound a lion makes," or "This character is from the book you read for your last book report."

Ask Me Anything . . .

Would your child rather be sprayed by a skunk or sleep outside in the rain? This activity can help you learn answers to some strange questions. Be careful what you ask—once your child answers five questions, it's your turn. Then you have to answer anything she asks you! Here are some questions to get the game started:

- ✦ What is your favorite orange food?
- ✦ If you could be an animal, what would you be?
- ✦ You have to rename everybody in the family based on a personality trait. What are their new names?
- ✦ Would you rather have super hearing or super vision?
- ✦ What's your most embarrassing moment?

Just remember, if you're going to ask about things like embarrassing moments, it's probably a good idea to set some rules about who this information can be shared with later!

Would you rather . . . ?

Artist on Board

Ask your child to find different words to describe a shade of a color. For example—shades of red. He might say "fire engine red," or "brick." Step in only when he is having trouble thinking of another shade. Then you can say "scarlet," or change to a new color.

What If the World Were Weirder?

Your child is probably used to waiting around because it happens commonly in our world. But if she's complaining about it, it's a good time to ask her to think about what would happen if the world were different. Can she tell you what a world with no waiting would look like? You can keep her thinking about different worlds by using some of these conversation starters.

What would we do if . . .
. . . trees could eat regular food?
. . . people could fly but not walk?
. . . dogs could talk?
. . . something else grew on trees rather than leaves?
. . . candy grew on the ground instead of grass?
. . . everything were a different color?
. . . it rained something else instead of water?
. . . people were born old and got younger every year?
. . . gravity pulled everything up instead of down?
. . . nobody ever got mad or sad?

BRAIN TEASER: WHERE SHOULD HE LIVE?

Test your child's brain game by asking him the following brain teaser:

If three friends moved to the same town, and one lived on E-X Avenue, while another lived on E-Y Road, where does the third one live?

Science and Measuring in Turn

This game is difficult, but it's great for older kids. Ask your child to list as many scientific rules as she can come up with before she runs out of ideas. For example, she might say, "There are twelve inches in a foot," or "Water freezes at 32°F and 0°C." If you're playing with young children, don't forget there are simpler rules to contribute, too, such as "There are seven days in a week."

VARIATION

Make the game a little more interesting by allowing your child to state made-up scientific rules. The challenge then becomes to see if you can guess if the rule is real or fake!

The Name Game

Has your child ever noticed that he has the same initials as other people even when they don't have the same name? If not, point it out to him! Once he's thought of a few other people who have the same initials as him, you can play the Name Game.

Begin the game by naming a famous person, such as George Washington. The next player uses the first initial of the last name (W) to start the first name of his person—Walt Disney, for example. The third player then comes up with a "D" name, such as Daniel Radcliffe.

VARIATION

Instead of using names, have your child use geography. In Geography, the last letter of the first word gives you the first letter of the next word. For example, Paris, then San Diego, then Ontario. To keep the game really moving, have your child reverse directions if the first and last letters are the same (as in Ontario).

Ghost

This game is one that the whole family can play together, but it can be just as much fun if it's just you and your child. To begin, the first person thinks of any word that's not a name—but doesn't tell anyone what it is.

Then he says the first letter out loud. The next family member adds a letter—and must be thinking of a real word that has that first and that second letter. The third person adds a letter, and makes sure the three letters do not spell a real word all on their own. They still have to be part of a longer real word. As the letters add up, it gets harder and harder to avoid spelling out a word!

For example, your child might be thinking of the word "plate." He starts by saying the letter *P*. Then you have to think of a word that starts with a *P* and add a letter to start spelling that word. If you're thinking of the word "pluto," you would say, "PL." Your child would then say, "PLA." You can't spell "pluto" any more, so you have to think of a new word, such as "player." You'd then say, "PLAY," but since that spells a real word, you lose the round and get the letter *G*. The first person who is forced to spell out a word (or who does so accidentally) gets the letter *G*. If a person is stuck and cannot think of a letter to add without spelling a word, that person may be tempted to "fake it" and say any letter that doesn't make a word. You can challenge that trickster—if she isn't thinking of a real word, then she gets a *G* also.

Once a word ends, the next person begins with a new word, and the game goes on. The first person to lose five times and spell out "GHOST" loses.

Foul Feast

This is definitely not a game to play with your child at the dinner table, because it can get *gross*ly out of hand! In this game, you and your child each contribute the name of two foods—so that together you have made up the most unpleasant food imaginable. Once you've settled on an appetizer, such as "fried slugs with mud dip," you can add to the menu by coming up with the main course or side dishes. Does "broccoli with swamp minnow sauce" go well with "boiled buffalo head," or should it be paired with "seared sandal salad?" And don't forget dessert! After all, your dinner isn't over until you've had the "snail sundae with chocolate sauce."

Animal Advantages

Ask your child to choose three traits from three different animals that can be combined to a make a superanimal. For example, perhaps your child wants to combine the speed of a cheetah, the swoop of an eagle, and the deep diving of a killer whale. Once she's decided on the traits that the superanimal will have, have her come up with a name for that superanimal. For example, the one described here could be the "Cheagle Whale." The catch is this—your child also has to explain why these combined traits would be useful. For example, a Cheagle Whale would never face extinction. It can swim so fast that it can get away from predators in the blink of an eye. And because it can dive deep in the ocean as well as swoop into the sky, finding food wouldn't be a problem in water or on land.

 Mythological Mix-Up

Does your child know that there were many of these combination animals in Greek and other mythologies? For instance, the centaur supposedly had the brains and chest of a person and the four legs and back of a horse. You can help him find images of these unusual creatures on the Internet if he can't picture what they would look like!

What's Your Animal?

What animal or animals would your child least like to be? Why? ("Swamp rat" and "desert scorpion" come to mind.) Of course, the flip side of these questions is what animals would your child really *like* to be and why? What animal does he think you would be if you were an animal instead of a person? And what about his brothers or sisters? What would they be?

How Does That Go Again?

A quick way to help your child to entertain herself while you're waiting is to have her create a new last line to a classic song or nursery rhyme, making sure it still rhymes with the line it's supposed to rhyme with. Here's an example:

Row, row, row your boat
Gently down the stream.
My brother isn't nearly as
much fun as he might seem.

Having trouble thinking of those classic nursery rhymes or songs? Here's a list to help you out!

◆ "Mary Had a Little Lamb"
◆ "Baa, Baa, Black Sheep"
◆ "Hickory, Dickory, Dock"
◆ "One, Two, Buckle My Shoe"
◆ "Twinkle, Twinkle Little Star"

If your child is having a hard time finding a rhyme, it's okay for her to use nonsense words or change the rhythm a little. The whole point is to have some fun!

Say! All These Sentences Sound the Same

Alliteration is when the same consonant is used at the beginning of the words in a sentence. Take turns making silly alliterative sentences that use your child's name. For example, if your child's name is Max, you might say something like, "Max's mom makes a monstrous mess on Monday mornings." When neither of you can think of any more alliterations for his name, choose a new one! This is a great activity that will keep your kid occupied whether you're waiting at the doctor's office, a restaurant, or more!

Name a New Kind of . . .

As your child looks around the waiting room, he may notice that some medications and medical companies have unusual names. Mention to him that they're often named for what they help or the people who invented them. What would he call a medicine he created to help with hiccups, for example? Here are some things your child can come up with a with a brand name for a new kind of . . .

. . . strawberry ice cream?
. . . soap?
. . . lemon ice cream?
. . . toothpaste?
. . . blueberry ice cream?
. . . deodorant?
. . . chocolate ice cream?

. . . shampoo?
. . . lemon pie?
. . . finger paint?
. . . butterscotch cake?
. . . TV set?
. . . granola cereal?

After he's named these new products, maybe he can come up with a few of his own. Can other people guess what the new product is based on the name he's created?

Three On-the-Go Ways to Use Wikki Stix

If you're not familiar with Wikki Stix, you should be! They're simply short strings of wax-covered yarn that can be bent into shapes and molded. Wikki Stix are a great way to keep kids entertained while giving them a non-messy way to play and fidget. Simply pop a package or two into your purse or to-go bag. There are any number of ways your child can use them. Here are three ideas to get you and your child started:

1. **Dot-to-dot pages:** Some packages already include mini dot-to-dot pages that your child can use, but she can also use them on any page in any activity book. All she has to do is press the end of a stick on the first dot, then move to the next dot, bending the Wikki Stix along the way. When she's done, she'll see the picture and be able to pull the sticks off the page. It makes the Wikki Stix *and* the activity page reusable!

2. **Window tic-tac-toe:** Your child can make play tic-tac-toe right on your car window. All she has to do is make the grid and then shape the rest of the Stix into Xs and Os. The wax may smudge the window, but a wiping with a paper towel will take it right off.

3. **Wax jewelry:** Have your child accessorize with her Wikki Stix. She can make rings, necklaces, bracelets, and more. Encourage her to be creative—maybe she can make a charm bracelet or a necklace with her name on it!

TECH IT UP A NOTCH

Dreamjob Kid's Doctor

This app takes your child on a 3D virtual tour of the doctor's entire office—from waiting room to exam room. After the tour, your child will start seeing patients and try to take care of them in a timely fashion. If she doesn't get to them in time, the other patients will leave before they are seen. (iOS, Android)

Rock, Paper, Scissors
(Lizard, Spock?)

When your child's feeling bored and he doesn't have anything with him to keep himself occupied, remind that he can play the classic game of Rock, Paper, Scissors without needing any supplies. Your child probably already knows how to play, but here's a brief recap of how to play. Each player makes a fist and chants, "Rock, Paper, Scissors," emphasizing each word by swinging his fist down. After the word "scissors," each player makes either a "rock," (closed fist), "paper," (an open hand, palm down) or "scissors," (a *V* with his index and middle fingers). Here's a breakdown of the rules:

- ◆ Rock breaks Scissors
- ◆ Scissors cut Paper
- ◆ Paper covers Rock

The winner is the player whose object beats the other ones.

VARIATION

Software developers Sam Kass and Karen Bryla created a version of this game called Rock, Paper, Scissors, Lizard, Spock. (Spock refers to a fictional character from *Star Trek*—a Vulcan who always proceeds with logic.) The hand gesture for Lizard looks like you're making a sock puppet mouth with your hand. Spock is the Vulcan salute, a *V* made by putting the index finger and middle finger together and moving them toward your thumb, and putting your ring finger and pinkie together.

The rules for this version are a little more complex (and a little more grim), but will definitely keep your child thinking.

- ◆ Scissors cut Paper
- ◆ Paper covers Rock
- ◆ Rock crushes Lizard
- ◆ Lizard poisons Spock
- ◆ Spock smashes Scissors
- ◆ Scissors decapitate Lizard
- ◆ Lizard eats Paper
- ◆ Paper disproves Spock
- ◆ Spock vaporizes Rock
- ◆ Rock crushes Scissors

Once your child learns this version of the game, he may never want to play the classic version again!

Waiting Room Spelling Bee

Holding a spelling bee in a waiting room can help you feel like you're using that time a little more productively. You may even want to hold a themed spelling bee, one in which your child spells words having to do with the type of office (stethoscope, thermometer, shot, nurse).

The rules are simple. Each player takes turns giving the other players a word to spell. If the first player spells it correctly, she chooses a word for the next player. If a player cannot spell a word, the word passes to the next person.

Don't forget to keep your child's ability and frustration level in mind when you choose words. Do you think your child can spell "sphygmomanometer?" If not, you might just want to use the more common phrase, "blood pressure cuff!" After all, if you're in a waiting room, there's a good chance one of you isn't feeling well to start with!

Exam Glove Puppets

If you've been stuck waiting in an exam room at the doctor's office, you may feel desperate for a way to entertain your child. All you need for this fun activity is a doctor's examination glove, a pair of scissors, and a pen. Cut the fingers off the gloves, put them on your child's fingers, then let your child use the pen or markers to create a face and other features.

TECH IT UP A NOTCH

Toca Doctor

This app gives your child the opportunity to see and take care of "patients." It has puzzles and games that help your child learn about the human body. The puzzles don't take very long, so it's a perfect app to play in the waiting room. (iOS)

Real Finger Puppets

Whether you're in a restaurant, waiting room, or even the dreaded DMV, all you need is a pen to keep your child entertained. Simply draw a face on each finger of your child's hand and have her use her fingers to create a play or act out a rhyme like "Little Miss Muffet" or "Little Jack Horner."

VARIATION

Jazz up this activity by taping some yarn, paper, or straw wrappers onto your child's fingers to create hair and clothing.

BRAIN TEASER: WHAT DOES THE CAT WANT?

Test your child's brain game by asking him the following brain teaser:

Just for fun, Cassie taught her cat Freddie sign language. One day the cat tapped on the window (a sign for "bird"), tapped his tail on the wall (a sign for "mouse"), and jumped into the tub to swim (a sign for "fish"). What was Freddie trying to tell Cassie?

Whatever You Do, Don't Laugh!

This game can be very funny, but if your child tends to have a hard time recovering from a case of the giggles, you may want to play in a noisy restaurant instead of in a quiet waiting room. To play, give your child a short phrase, such as "dad's pajamas." Then ask him questions that he has to answer using that phrase. The goal is to see if he can keep a straight face as he answers. Here are some questions you can use:

+ What did you eat for breakfast?
+ What do you brush your hair with?
+ Who helped you with your homework?
+ What do your wear when it rains?

When he laughs, the next player (you, another child, etc.) is "it," and uses a new phrase. Here are some phrases you can use:

+ A horse's tail
+ My mother's moustache
+ Seven stinky monsters
+ A smelly shoe
+ Your sister's toothbrush

The next time you're waiting in a restaurant, you may not even need to suggest this game. You can just say, "Did you eat dad's pajamas for breakfast?" and watch your child get the giggles!

TECH IT UP A NOTCH

Fruit Ninja

This app has more to do with fruit than ninjas. And it doesn't even have that much to do with fruit! Your child uses her finger as a sword of sorts to just slice and dice fruit. The better she gets, well, the better she gets. (iOS, Android)

RESTAURANT SCAVENGER HUNT

You don't want your child to get up and wander around a restaurant, but her eyes still can. Challenge her to find restaurant-related items as you wait to be seated or for your food to arrive. Here's a list to get her started:

☐ Sign that has the word "please" on it

☐ TV showing the news/sports/cartoons

☐ Someone wearing an apron

☐ Family with three kids

☐ Four menu items containing cheese

☐ Condiment that is not ketchup

☐ EXIT sign

☐ Menu item that costs less than $3.49

☐ Fire extinguisher

☐ Fake flowers or plant

☐ Real flowers or plant

☐ Picture or description of a dessert that does not have chocolate in it

☐ Somebody with red/brown/blonde hair

Once you run out of ideas, switch the game up. Have your child challenge you to find the items she names!

The Straw Wrapper Worm

This cool trick only requires straws with a paper covering and a few drops of liquid. Ask your server for a handful of extra straws. Help your child remove the straw wrappers by slowly pushing them down accordion-style from the top of the straw to the bottom. That squished straw wrapper is about to become a wiggling worm!

Put the straw wrapper on the table or on a laminated menu. Have your child dip the tip of his straw into his drink glass. Then, have him put a finger over the top end of the straw to create a vacuum. He only needs a few drops of liquid, so the idea is to draw up just a little bit in the bottom of the straw.

Keeping his finger over the top of the straw, have him remove it from his glass and position it over the squished-up wrapper. Tell him to slowly move his finger and let one drop at a time fall. As the liquid is absorbed, the paper wiggles forward like an inchworm!

Please Pass the Checkers

You can play checkers at the restaurant using whatever is handy at your table. All you'll need is a paper napkin, a crayon, and a few sugar packets or other small condiments.

Ask for an extra paper napkin. It's probably already folded into a rectangle. Fold again so you have a tall, skinny rectangle. Open the napkin up all the way and have your child carefully trace the folds with a crayon (if you have one). You may need to help, since the napkin can tear easily. The napkin should now have seven lines and be divided into eight columns.

Fold the napkin back into its original shape and place so the original crease is running sideways. Fold up to make a long, skinny rectangle. Open and trace the new fold lines. You have a checkerboard!

Grab the sweetener packets, set the board with twelve packets of one color and twelve packets of a different color, and start playing checkers. If you don't have enough packets, you can always have your child politely ask the next table over if you can borrow some sugar.

TECH IT UP A NOTCH

Smash Your Food

Your child probably loves playing with her food nearly as much as you hate watching her do it. This app allows for the best of both worlds—your child gets to virtually play with her food while also learning about nutrition. She has to choose from a menu of foods and then guess how much sugar, salt, and fat they contain. As she guesses, the food is served onto a plate, put in a vise, and smashed, complete with explosions and squishy food noises. (iOS)

Jelly Packet Jenga

Your child probably already plays with the jelly packets and butter pats at restaurants during breakfast time, so why not keep her extra busy and make a game of it?

To begin, help your child build a tower. Use two jelly packets on the bottom and then alternate between one and two packets for each level after that.

Next, each person around the table takes a turn pulling a packet from the middle of the tower, trying hard not to knock the whole thing down. The game may not take long, but it will be fun while it lasts.

TECH IT UP A NOTCH

Awesome Eats

In this app, your child sorts and stacks garden-fresh food to create a plate to pack. She also helps the food travel through some innovative contraptions while shooing away birds. After "lunch," your child can also recycle to earn more points. (iOS)

SEAFOOD WORD SEARCH

If you're eating a seafood restaurant, you can probably look around and see a number of things (either out the window or on the walls) that remind you of the coast. In this word grid, see if your child can find thirteen things you might see when eating at a seafood restaurant. The words can go backward, forward, up, down, and diagonally.

BRIDGE
BUOY
FISHERMEN
KITES
LIFEGUARDS

LIGHTHOUSE
LOBSTER POT
ROWBOAT
SAILBOAT
SAND

SEAGULL
SURFERS
WAVES

```
S  S  S  A  I  L  B  O  A  T  S
L  D  E  E  G  D  I  R  B  E  L
O  R  R  T  S  H  E  S  V  I  L
B  O  E  A  I  L  L  A  G  S  L
S  W  S  E  U  K  W  H  A  S  U
T  B  H  E  L  G  T  L  S  B  G
E  O  Y  T  S  H  E  Y  H  E  A
R  A  S  A  O  E  A  F  O  S  E
P  T  N  U  H  O  R  E  I  U  S
O  D  S  U  R  F  E  R  S  L  B
T  E  F  I  S  H  E  R  M  E  N
```

Extra puzzle points: After your child has circled all the listed words, have her read the leftover letters from left to right, and top to bottom, to find a popular tongue twister!

Coaster Hockey

This game works best at a restaurant that has the perfect combination of cardboard coasters and a slippery table surface. Have the players (you and your child, etc.) sit across the table from each other. Each should place a butter knife horizontally on the table in front of them to act as a goal post.

Clear the path between the goals, give each player a coaster to use as a paddle, and put another one in the middle as a puck. The object is to use the paddles to knock the puck into your opponent's goal post. The game ends when someone gets to five "goals"—or when your meal arrives.

TECH IT UP A NOTCH

Toca Kitchen 2

Your child gets to be the chef in charge with this app. There aren't any puzzles to solve in the Toca Kitchen. You child simply chooses a character, opens the fridge, and finds things to feed to her character. She can cut, cook, boil, fry, microwave, or use a food processor to prepare the food. The best part is getting to see your child react to how each character responds to the food she tries to feed him! (iOS, Android)

Dancing Raisins

Your child probably doesn't know that raisins can dance. Add a few snack-sized boxes to your purse or pocket and you can show him the next time you're at a restaurant. While you're waiting for your food, ask your server to bring a glass of clear soda without ice—ginger ale, Sprite, or tonic water all work well. Give your child a few raisins to pop in the cup and he can watch them dance from the bottom to the top and back again.

HOW HUNGRY ARE YOU?

Your restless, hungry kid probably knows what "McD's" stands for, but does she know what these acronyms stand for? Here are a couple of hints you can give her to help.

1. She might order this food at lunchtime or for a light meal.

2. If she's *really* hungry, she may ask the server to bring her food in this speedy manner.

BLT

ASAP

B _____

L _____

T _____

A _____

S _____

A _____

P _____

Who's That?

Ask your child to think of somebody you both know. It can be a friend or a relative, but not a celebrity. (Unless your friends or relatives are celebrities!) Ask her to provide you with a hint. For instance, "He has a mustache." Then you should try to guess who your child is thinking of. If nobody can guess the person, your child has to keep adding more specific clues, such as "He always chews gum."

BRAIN TEASER: WHY IS SHE LOSING TIME?

Test your child's brain game by asking him the following brain teaser!

Beth has an unusual talent. She can walk backward for miles. Some days she even walks to school backward. If it takes her longer to get there, how much farther is it to school?

Twenty Questions

Twenty Questions is a great game for when you're waiting around. It's also a great way to harness your child's fondness for asking endless questions! All you have to do is think of a noun. Your child can start by asking the classic question, "Animal, mineral, or vegetable?" She then can ask nineteen additional yes or no questions in order to figure out what you're thinking of. The object is to guess it in fewer than twenty questions.

Fake Excuses

While you're waiting at the doctor's office, see if your child can think of ridiculous excuses as to why he's not at school today. You can start by saying something like, "I'm sorry John isn't in school today. He lost a tooth last night and is spending all day looking for it!" Let your child's imagination run wild and laugh at how inventive your child can be!

Who Am I?

Similar to Twenty Questions, this is a great game to quietly play with your child while you wait. To start, have your child think of an animal. She shouldn't tell you what she's chosen. Instead of asking yes or no questions out loud, you try to guess the animal by either making animal noises or by acting out motions that various animals may do. For example, if you're trying to guess "cat," you could meow or pretend to lick your "paws" and "wash" your face.

What Do These Words Have in Common?

This game is sometimes known as the Game of Threes. Have your child think of three words that have something in common. The commonality doesn't have to be obvious. In fact, the less obvious it is, the more challenging the game is. The rest of the players have to figure out what the words have in common. Here are some word trios to get you started.

- ✦ Volkswagen-ladybug-John Lennon (beetles/Beatles)
- ✦ Christmas-business-deck (cards)
- ✦ toes-heel-ankle (parts of a foot)
- ✦ racket-net-ball (items needed for tennis)

What's My Word?

Have each member of your family write five words on small pieces of paper. These words are the "secret passwords." One player chooses a slip from somebody else's pile. He then has to use clue words to try to get other players to guess the "secret password." The only catch is that he can't use the word or any variation of it as part of the clue!

Celebrity

To play this game, have each player write a celebrity name on a small piece of paper. You may have to write more than one so that there are at least five slips of paper. Put all the slips in a pile and have one person choose a celebrity name. That player then has to give hints about the celebrity to see if people can guess who it is. He can use hints like, "This name sounds like . . . " but he cannot use the name or a variation of it as part of the clue.

VARIATION

Have each player use pantomime (no words allowed!) to give hints.

Mirror, Mirror

Does your child mimic every move you make? If so, this activity is a perfect way to pass some time while you're waiting around. Face each other and pretend you are mirror images of each other. One person makes a movement, such as licking his lips, smiling, or yawning. The other person has to mimic it as quickly as possible so that it looks like a reflection in a mirror. If you're standing up, your movements can be more complicated—as long as you're not bothering the people around you!

Taste Test

Does your child play with all the condiments on the table at a restaurant? Instead of constantly telling him to "put the salt shaker down already," put those condiments to use for entertainment. Ask your server for an extra spoon or two and do a condiment taste test! Have your child close his eyes, put a little ketchup or sweetener on the spoon, and ask him to identify what he's tasting. Is it sweet, salty, bitter, or sour?

TECH IT UP A NOTCH

205 Sounds

This Android app tests your child's ability to identify everyday noises from animals to instruments.

What's That Sound?

Can your child identify sounds with his eyes closed? It's easy enough to find out! Have your child shut his eyes tight and test his ears by making a noise and asking him to guess what it was. Some ideas to consider:

✦ Clinking silverware on a glass (carefully!)
✦ Pushing your chair away from the table
✦ Jiggling pocket change
✦ Dropping a penny in a cup
✦ Dropping your keys on the floor
✦ Clucking your tongue

Once you run out of ideas of sounds to make, ask your child to listen to the sounds of the busy restaurant. Can she identify the noises other people are making?

BRAIN TEASER:
CAN YOU READ BETWEEN THE NUMBERS?

Test your child's brain game by asking him the following brain teaser:

What would happen if you 8 and 8?

FRIGHTENED FOOD

This puzzle may not keep your hungry child's mind off food, but it will keep her occupied while she's waiting! Hand her this book and have her highlight each of the thirty foods stuffed into this letter grid. Remind her words can go sideways, up and down, diagonal, and even backward. After she has found them all, have her collect the unused letters from TOP to BOTTOM and LEFT to RIGHT, and write them in order on the blank spaces provided. When she's finished, she will have the answer to this riddle: *What has bread on both sides and is easy to frighten?*

Variation: Have your child use three different colors of crayons or markers to show her answers!

APPLE
BEET
BLINTZ
BREAD
BROWNIES
CAKE
CARROT
CHEESE
CLAM
EGG
HAMBURGER
HOTDOG
JELLY
KIWI
MILK
ORANGE
PEA
PEANUT BUTTER
PEAR
PEPPER
PIE
PIZZA
PLUM
PORK
RADISH
SALAD
SPAGHETTI
TUNA FISH
TURKEY
YAM

What has bread on both sides and is easy to frighten?

S	P	A	G	H	E	T	T	I	E	I	P
E	G	N	A	R	O	U	A	P	P	L	E
A	B	C	S	E	I	N	W	O	R	B	A
C	L	A	M	P	Y	A	M	R	C	E	N
H	I	K	R	L	I	F	K	K	C	E	U
K	N	E	A	U	M	I	L	K	C	T	T
A	T	E	E	M	W	S	A	L	A	D	B
P	Z	U	P	I	H	H	J	G	R	C	U
E	N	Z	R	S	D	S	E	O	R	H	T
P	A	N	I	K	A	D	L	D	O	E	T
P	W	D	I	P	E	C	L	T	T	E	E
E	A	G	G	E	R	Y	Y	O	H	S	R
R	E	G	R	U	B	M	A	H	P	E	A

__ _____ _____!

Handy Dandy

This activity is perfect to play with younger children while you're waiting around. First, show your child both of your hands, then place a small object such as a coin, a sweetener packet, or a piece of candy in one of your hands. Then, put your hands behind your back and tell your child that you are moving the object from hand to hand. Close your hands into fists and bring them back to the front of your body. Hold one hand higher than the other. Then recite the following poem and ask your child to guess which hand is holding the object:

Handy dandy midley moe
Which do you pick, the high or the low?

When your child picks the correct hand, you can either give her the object to keep or let her take a turn at hiding it in her hands.

Cotton Cash

If you're struggling to keep your child entertained in a restaurant or waiting room, just pull a dollar bill out of your wallet and let your child explore. Tell your child that U.S. bills are made of 75 percent cotton and that, when the cotton fibers are processed, they become very strong. Have her hold the bill up to the light and see if she can see the individual fibers.

Then, have her tell you what else she sees on the bill. What symbols does she see? What type of watermarks or counterfeit protections are visible on the bill? With any luck, your child will be staring at the bill until it's time to use it to tip your waitress or pay the copay!

SECOND HELPINGS

If your child is antsy while you're waiting for your food to arrive at a restaurant or if she's finished eating before you, pass the book over to her and let her solve this Second Helpings puzzle. Tell her that each food name in the puzzle has at least one set of double letters in it that have been left in the puzzle to help her out.

ACROSS

3. Smooth and creamy dessert served in a bowl
5. Hot tomato and cheese pie served in triangles
7. Breakfast food covered with little squares
8. Sometimes this is inside a roast chicken
11. Creamy drink made in a blender from milk, fruit, and ice
12. This gets sliced on pizza or tossed in salads
15. Fluffy, sweet, and golden bread made with many eggs
17. Italian pasta you twirl on a fork
19. Prickly golden fruit with stiff green leaves on top
24. Small, round fruits that grow on bushes
25. Leafy vegetable used to make salads
26. A sweet treat eaten after a meal
27. Dark-colored soda that's not cola
28. Fragrant spice often used in Christmas cookies

DOWN

1. Tasty dip made from chickpeas
2. Long, flat pasta made from flour and egg
4. Hard, golden candy made from butter, sugar, and cream
6. These long, green vegetables grow like crazy in the summer
9. Sweet treats made on a stick
10. Mexican flatbread used to wrap around food
12. Small breakfast cakes
13. Cooked spheres of hamburger, egg, and spices
14. Round, flat, baked treats
16. Mervin loves this dairy product that's sometimes sliced and sometimes stretchy.

18. Crunchy Chinese "tube" filled with vegetables and meat
20. Vegetable that looks like a tree
21. Dairy product you can melt or spread
22. Round, red vegetables that grow underground
23. Small, round, red fruits with long stems

SOUP'S ON!

Sometimes a hot bowl of soup is the best restaurant appetizer you can order! If you and your child are waiting for some soup to warm the two of you up on a chilly day, hand her this book and have her take a look at the very strange items that have fallen into each of the soup bowls. Have her cross out the ingredients that she would never find in soup, then have her see if she can figure out what kind of soup is in each pot!

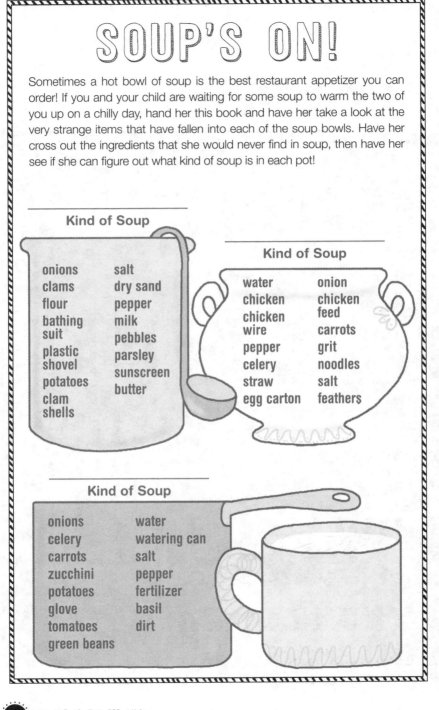

Kind of Soup _____

onions
clams
flour
bathing suit
plastic shovel
potatoes
clam shells
salt
dry sand
pepper
milk
pebbles
parsley
sunscreen
butter

Kind of Soup _____

water
chicken
chicken wire
pepper
celery
straw
egg carton
onion
chicken feed
carrots
grit
noodles
salt
feathers

Kind of Soup _____

onions
celery
carrots
zucchini
potatoes
glove
tomatoes
green beans
water
watering can
salt
pepper
fertilizer
basil
dirt

Origami Dog

Want to impress your child while you're waiting for your food at a restaurant? All you need is a napkin and some folding skills. Take a paper napkin and tear it so it's square, then fold it in half to make a triangle. Fold it in half again, then unfold it. With the open end facing down, fold the other two corners down to make the ears. Fold the bottom corner back to make a chin. Then, if you have a pen, hand your creation over to you child and let her draw on a face and give the dog a name! If you have an older child, let her do the steps along with you while you wait!

The Laughing Test

Has your child ever heard the phrase "laughter is contagious?" Explain to her what it means—that when someone else laughs, it's almost impossible not to laugh yourself. Then set her loose to test the theory. She can use a mobile device to record you laughing or to pull up a video of her favorite funny vlogger. Does she laugh every time she hears the recording? What happens if she plays it for her friends or siblings?

Since you're waiting around anyway, she may even be able to give other people the laughing test. Challenge her to see happens when you and your family get a case of the giggles, make funny faces, or tell ridiculous jokes. Do the people around you smile or laugh with you?

Chapter 5

•••••••••••••••

SHOPPING TRIP GAMES

Shopping with your kids on hand can be challenging, to say the least. Sometimes it can be downright overwhelming to manage protests of boredom, requests for bathroom breaks, and all the extra items that were furtively dropped in the shopping cart when you turned your head. In this chapter, you'll find a variety of fun activities that will help keep your kids entertained while you get your shopping done. After all, if you can't keep your kids calm, you definitely want to keep them busy!

Musical Parody

If your child isn't familiar with parodies, pull up Weird Al or the latest viral video on your mobile device and show him one. Your younger child may find it easier to relate to *Sesame Street*'s parodies. Once he understands the idea of a parody, encourage him to make up one of his own. He doesn't actually have to make a video; it can be just for your family's amusement.

Choose a topic, such as "dogs" or "your favorite movie." Challenge everybody to make a song about that topic to the tune of a familiar song. Part of the fun is guessing which song each person started with!

What's the Best Superpower?

If your child could have one superpower, what would it be? Ask her to tell you why it's the best superpower and what she would use it for. What would her superhero name be? Who is her archenemy and what powers does he have?

Once you've started talking superpowers, don't forget to talk about the downsides, too. After all, it might seem cool to be able to read minds, but what if somebody is thinking mean things about you?

BRAIN TEASER: HOW CAN HE EAT SO MUCH?

Test your child's brain game by asking him the following brain teaser!

When Toby's family entered the Yummyville eating contest, Toby was amazed when his little brother won the prize for swallowing over 1,000 items in 2 minutes. Do you know how he did it?

Alphabetically Speaking

Choose a letter of the alphabet and have your child say a sentence using a word that begins with that letter. The next person has to begin his sentence with a word that starts with the next letter in the alphabet. The tricky thing is that you have to be having a conversation, not just saying random sentence. For example:

Have you eaten kiwi before?
I have and I didn't like it!
Jeez, I love kiwi.
Kiwi has too many seeds in it.
Little seeds, though.
Makes my tongue feel funny.
Nevertheless, I'm going to buy some kiwi.
Okay.

You can even challenge your child to see if he can help you keep the conversation going for your entire shopping trip!

Are You Questioning Me?

In this game you and your child can only talk in questions, but you have to be having a real conversation. And don't let your child get away with trying to disguise a statement as a question! That means no questions that start with phrases like, "Doesn't it seem as though . . . ?" Your conversation might sound like this:

Have you seen that new movie?
No, have you?
Who would I have gone with?
Didn't Dad want to see it?
Did he say he wanted to see it?
Didn't you hear him tell me that last week?

The downside of teaching your child this game is that he may try to play it when you don't want him to speak in questions!

Are You a Birdbrain?

Do you dare call your child a birdbrain? Just be prepared to let him know it's really not what it sounds like! Have each person name a bird until no one can think of one that hasn't been said. You can all decide whether to set a time limit for a person to come up with one. Use your judgment. Obviously, a player can't take more than a minute to think of "blue jay" or something easy, but as the game goes on, though, you may want to allow a little more time to think of rare birds. When you start *feeling* like a birdbrain, it might be time to switch to dog breeds!

School Supplies 101

When it's time to go back-to-school shopping, your child may have a list to work from, but it doesn't always include everything she might need. Keep your child engaged during your trip by asking her if she can name things that people use as school supplies. She can probably think of the small, common items (like pens and pencils), but she may not be able to name all of the big things (like a desk) that are needed if you're the teacher or are going to college.

When she starts to get stuck, remind her to think of what she carries in her book bag, what her teacher might have on his desk, or the things she uses every day that a college student might need for a dorm room (like soap or a trashcan).

BRAIN TEASER: THAT'S A HOLE LOTTA FOOD!

Test your child's brain game by asking him the following brain teaser!

When Ben and his father went to the grocery store, his father asked him if he could find four foods in the store that had holes in them but that were still whole. Ben found more than four. How many can you think of?

Buy One, Get Won

Make or print a couple of charts listing the numbers from one to one hundred in rows. Then, while you're shopping have your child keep her eyes open for numbers and number words at the store. For example, she may see a "Buy One, Get One Free" sign or fruit for $3.29 per pound. Each time she sees a number, she should color it in on her chart or circle it with the pen you probably have on hand for your shopping list. When you get home, see how many numbers she found in the store.

Sentence Rhyme

See if your child can come up with a long sentence in which all the major words rhyme with every other. It doesn't necessarily even have to make sense. For example, "Ted and Fred said to shed your head or end up wedding the undead." Can your child start a rhyming sentence using the name of one of the items in the store?

TECH IT UP A NOTCH

Daisy the Dinosaur

This is a game for the youngest of beginning coders. There's a challenge mode and a free play mode. In both modes, your child will play with basic commands like "move," "jump," and "spin" to make Daisy the dinosaur move around the screen. (iOS, Android)

Grocery Gumshoe

The next time you stop in a grocery store you don't typically go to, it's a good chance for your child to snoop around like a "grocery gumshoe." Let your child nose around the deli counter, fish counter, and bakery areas. Ask him: What do they sell here that you don't typically see in our usual store? For instance, some stores (and areas) are known for their seafood or special fruits and vegetables. It's always interesting to see what's "normal" for other stores, and sometimes it's nice to think about what's special about your home store, too!

 ## What's a Gumshoe?

The word "gumshoe" dates back about a hundred years, to when people wore a type of soft-soled rubber shoe, called a gumshoe, that allowed them to walk around quietly.

To Tell You the Truth

In this game, each player takes a turn saying three sentences—two of which are true and one of which is not. The other players have to guess which one is not true. For example, you might start off the game by saying, "I love shopping with you. I forgot to bring the coupons. I don't like going to the grocery store on the weekend." Keep in mind your three sentences don't have to be grocery-store specific. You can say anything you want to keep your kid guessing. The question is still the same: Which one of those isn't true? That's for your child to figure out.

VARIATION

Mix up this game by telling short stories about your day instead. The other players have to guess which things really happened and which did not.

Word Hot Potato

Have your child pick a topic, such as types of flowers or cartoon characters. Each person has to name something that fits in that topic. Each player names something as quickly as he can after the other player has said something. For example, you might say "roses," and your child might say "daffodils." The first person to pause drops the figurative "hot potato" and loses the game.

Salad Time

How many vegetables can your child name? She's probably able to think of many of the more common ones, like carrots, celery, and lettuce, but can she think of less commonly known vegetables like turnips and parsnips? And does she know which food botanists call a fruit and cooks call a vegetable? (Tomatoes.) This is a great activity to play while you're shopping in the produce section. That way if your child is having trouble thinking of a variety of vegetables, all she has to do is look around her. Who knows, she may even be inspired to try some new vegetables!

VARIATION

Once she's made a vegetable "salad," see if she can make a fruit salad, too! Remind her that some people also add other ingredients to a fruit salad. Maybe her fruit salad would include cheese or coconut shreds, too!

Can You Think of a Hink Pink?

Hink Pinks are riddles to which the answer is two one-syllable rhyming words. For example, you might ask your child, "What do you call a large hog?" The answer, of course, is a "big pig!"

See how many Hink Pinks you and your child can think up while you're shopping. Here are some ideas of Hink Pinks to get you started:

- ◆ What do you drive on the sun? *A star car.*
- ◆ What do you call a sad circus performer? *A down clown.*
- ◆ What do you call a spook who throws a party? *A ghost host.*
- ◆ Where do rodents live? *In a mouse house.*

Here's a hint if your child is having trouble thinking of Hink Pinks. It's sometimes easier to think of the second half, then find a descriptive word that rhymes and then come up with the question.

For example, your child can start with the word "lion," and then think of something silly that rhymes with it, like "cryin'." Then he can create a riddle to which the answer is "cryin' lion," such as "What do you call a sad king of the jungle?"

VARIATION

When you can't think of any more Hink Pinks, move on to a Hinky Pinky—two-syllable words that rhyme. Here are some Hinky Pinky ideas to get you started:

- ◆ What do cold cats wear on their hands? *Kitten's mittens.*
- ◆ What does a rabbit pay with? *Bunny money.*
- ◆ What do you call a silly rabbit? *A funny bunny.*
- ◆ What do you call a wet amphibian? *A soggy froggy.*
- ◆ What do you call a smelly little finger? *A stinky pinky.*

If your child is really good at word play, you may even want to try your hand at some three-syllable words that rhyme—Hinkety Pinketys!

WHO PARKED WHERE?

Keep your waiting child from getting impatient as you load your purchases into the car. Hand him this book and something to write with and have him solve this parking lot riddle!

Three cars are parked next to each other in a parking lot. By reading the clues that follow, can your child tell which people are going to get into which vehicle, the color of the vehicle, and what state they are from?

HINT: He can use the grid provided to help him figure out the answers.

- **The man with a dog is not in a silver truck and is not from New York.**
- **The blue vehicle is not from Maine.**
- **The family in the red vehicle is not from Maine or Ohio.**
- **The twin sisters are in a truck with a Maine license plate.**
- **The sports car is from New York.**
- **The van is not silver or red.**

	vehicle	state	color
man with dog			
twin sisters			
family			

Weirdo Country

When you're standing on line, try something new to distract your child from the candy and toys in the checkout lane. Ask him to think about creating a new country in which kids can buy whatever they want at the register. If your child *could* create a completely new country, what else would it be like? For instance, maybe it rains sunflower seeds, dogs only eat trash, all the trees are purple, and the parents are smaller than children. What would he name it?

BRAIN TEASER: HOW DID DAD KNOW?

Test your child's brain game by asking him the following brain teaser!

When Marty's dad asked him if he had been taking out the trash like he was supposed to, he answered, "Yes, I look at the moon every night I go out." Of course his father knew this was a lie. Why?

It's Like a Simile

See how many similes—a phrase that compares how one thing is like another—your child can think of based on the items around you. This is a good way to exercise your child's imagination, which means her comparisons don't have to be too literal. To help her get started, share the following comparison:

The clouds today are like . . . a scoop of vanilla ice cream, or a puddle of spilled milk.

TECH IT UP A NOTCH

Mad Libs

This app takes the classic road game and makes it digital. No more writing down nouns, verbs, or adjectives—your child can simply type them in as you say them and let autocorrect help. The app provides hints along the way and is refreshingly ad-free. (iOS)

Grocery Bingo

Grocery Bingo doesn't actually have to be a game that your child plays to win. Instead, he can simply look for all of the items on his card as you shop your way through the store.

You can make your own bingo card using grocery flyers and your shopping list. Your child just has to cross off each item as you put it in your cart. Or, if you prefer, you can search, download, and print a Grocery Store Bingo card from the Internet (or try *www .louisvillefamilyfun.net/2012/06/grocery-store-supermarket-bingo .html*).

I Spy

I Spy is a classic shopping trip game that is really easy to play. Here, one person looks around and chooses something in her line of sight. (You may have to let your child know that once she picks an item, she can't change it!)

Then she gives a clue, such as "I spy with my little eye something that starts with B." She could also give a clue as to the shape, color, or location of the object. However, unlike Twenty Questions, in this game, she doesn't continue to give clues to make it easier. Instead, you just have to look around and keep guessing items that fit your child's description. If you give up, your child chooses a new item. If you guess it, it's your turn to choose!

PARKING LOT

The following code is called a "parking lot code" because each letter is parked in a space that has a unique shape.

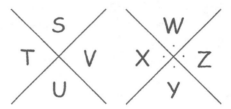

To send a message, have your child draw the outline of the parking space each letter is in, including the dot if there is one. For example, here is how to send the message "LOOK AT THAT."

L O O K   A T   T H A T !

Can you decipher this secret message? HINT: Your child may hear this a lot on a long trip!

Guess the Secret Word

In this activity, you and your child should take turns choosing a secret word. The word doesn't matter as much as your child's ability to keep talking about that word. It's her job to see how long it takes you to guess the secret word. (If she chooses a word like "shirt," it will be much easier to talk about than the word "arugula.")

Next, the first player has to decide on another word to substitute for the chosen word and begin a conversation that uses the secret word. As he's talking, the guesser has to try to figure out what the secret word is.

For instance, if the secret word is "shirt," and the substitute word is "abracadabra," the conversation might go something like this:

"John bought a new abracadabra at the mall today. All the abracadabras were on sale for two for $15. That's a good deal, but they had to be the same kind of abracadabras. He couldn't buy a short-sleeve one and a long-sleeve for $15 . . ."

BRAIN TEASER: WHAT KIND OF FRUIT SALAD IS THIS?

Test your child's brain game by asking him the following brain teaser:

One day Katherine decided to make a picture out of food, just for fun. First she used strawberries, then oranges, then lemons, then kiwis, then blueberries, and then another fruit. What did she use last and why?

Title Mashup

Does your child know all the names of popular songs, movies, books, and TV shows? This activity puts that knowledge to use and asks him to be a critical thinker, too. He makes a mashup of two titles, but doesn't reveal it. Instead, he has to give you a clue that uses elements of both. Then you guess the new name. For example:

This made-for-TV movie is about a young Viking dragon hunter who meets a dragon named Cassie and her friends Max and Emmy. (The answer is *How to Train Your Dragon Tales*.)

Look for Opposites and Synonyms

Choose a word and then ask your child to name as many antonyms (opposites) as she can. For instance, if you said "slow," your child might say "fast, quick, speedy." When she runs out of opposites, ask her to name synonyms for the original word. Here are some words to get you started:

- ✦ quiet
- ✦ happy
- ✦ pull
- ✦ expensive
- ✦ ask

Shop the Alphabet

Give your child a small notebook and a pen or open a note-taking app on your mobile device. As you shop for the things on your list, task your child with "shopping" for items for all the letters of the alphabet. As she finds something to match each letter, she can write it down. It's up to you to decide whether she should "shop" in alphabetical order, but doing it out of order may make your shopping trip easier!

VARIATION

Have your child find words that start or end with each letter of the alphabet. It might be simpler to find a word that uses the letter Z on price tags or store sign than to find an item that starts with Z!

BRAIN TEASER: WHAT DOESN'T BELONG?

Test your child's brain game by asking him the following brain teaser:

What doesn't belong in this list?
Pen, paper, spatula, notebook.

Favorites

Help pass the time in the grocery store by engaging your child with this simple game. Take turns being the leader with your child. The leader names a category like television shows, ice cream, or flowers. Then you and your child take turns listing your favorite things (in order) in that category.

Grocery Store Hunt

When you're in the grocery store, go into the coffee aisle and see how many countries your child can find that are mentioned in the coffee labels. Can she find coffee from Ethiopia? Columbia? Brazil? Can she find coffee that's grown in the United States? Hint: Hawaii is currently the only U.S. state that is able to grow coffee, but Georgia will begin harvesting soon.

BRAIN TEASER: THE DIRTY DISHES DILEMMA

Test your child's brain game by asking him the following brain teaser!

Jack has a lot of dishes to do. He has enough dishes to fill four sinks, and it takes him ten minutes to wash one sink full of dishes, five minutes to rinse, and five minutes to dry. How much time would it save him if he waited and rinsed all the dishes at the end (ten minutes total), and let them all air-dry?

Telling Tongue Twisters

Can your child say "Tommy tied twenty tiny tennis shoes," five times fast? If she can do that tongue twister, she's probably ready to make up a few of her own to entertain you and the rest of the family. Here are some hints to share with her for making new tongue twisters.

+ Have her pick a consonant (this tongue twister, for example, uses the letter *t*). Then ask her to try to come up with a bunch of words with that consonant. For instance, if she picks the consonant *d*, she might say, "Donny's dog didn't dig in the dirt."
+ Have her start with her name. Then she can answer the following questions with a word that starts with the same letter or rhymes with her name. What is she doing? Where, when, and why? Here's an example: "Sally sang a silly song on a sailboat in September because Sally likes the sunshine."

Before you know it, you and your child will be cracking up and your shopping will be finished, too!

Do You Know Your ZYXs?

Can your child say the alphabet backward? It's not as easy as it sounds! Pass him this book if he needs to see the letters in order to do it. It goes like this: Z, Y, X, W, V, U, T, S, R, Q, P, O, N, M, L, K, J, I, H, G, F, E, D, C, B, and A.

Once he's confident he remembers the letters in reverse order, time him saying them. How long does it take him to recite the alphabet backward? Can he do it in under a minute?

VARIATION

Add an extra twist and have him listen to the store's music while he does it. Does he notice that it's harder to concentrate with background noise?

 **One Long Word**

Pull up the classic *Sesame Street* song "ABC-DEF-GHI" on your mobile device. Your child may get a giggle out of Big Bird thinking the alphabet is one long word! Here's the link: *www.sesamestreet.org/videos?video=faafe1b6-b4f4-4c4d-a8ec-4909802eef81*

BRAIN TEASER:
WHAT DO THEY HAVE IN COMMON?

Test your child's brain game by asking him the following brain teaser:

What do the words "end," "multiplication," "kitchen," and "coffee" have in common? Hint: They're all adjectives for one noun.

Chapter 6

....

BONUS ACTIVITIES FOR WORK-FROM-HOME DAYS

While you definitely need to find ways to keep your kids occupied when you're out and about, as a parent, there will certainly be times when you need to entertain them at home, too. After all, it can be challenging to meet deadlines or make phone calls with your kids running around, and you don't want them to spend all day sitting in front of a screen. With some planning, you can do the activities in this chapter while you're in a hotel or on vacation, but they're great to use when your kids have the day off and you have to work. These fun activities are guaranteed to keep screen time to a minimum and imagination at a maximum.

Uh, What?

If you can trust your child to be nearby and quiet while you're on a conference call, let him count how many times people use placeholder sounds and words when they speak. Some words and sounds for him to listen for include:

- ◆ Uh . . .
- ◆ Umm . . .
- ◆ Uh-huh . . .
- ◆ Right . . .
- ◆ I see . . .

- ◆ You know . . .
- ◆ I think . . .
- ◆ Yeah . . .
- ◆ So . . .

When you're all done with work, ask your child to show you his tally list. It can be surprising how many times people say these words in just half an hour—including you!

Conference Calls

Keep your child occupied while you're on a conference call by letting her have one of her own. Make an appointment ahead of time to video chat with one of her friends or a tech-savvy grandparent. While you're talking over your latest project, your child can use a tablet or computer to show off hers to Grandma.

TECH IT UP A NOTCH

Cookie Calls or Elmo Calls

If your child is too young to do a live call without your help, download an app like Sesame Street's Cookie Calls or Elmo Calls at *www.sesamestreet .org/parents/apps*. Your child can practice her phone skills by "video chatting" with Cookie Monster or answering voicemails from Elmo! (iOS, Android)

What Else Could You Use It For?

When your child says she's bored, it's a good time to have her look at her surroundings in a different light. Right now, the bookshelf in her room is just a place to hold books and toys, but what else could it be used for? Maybe each shelf is a bed for a little elf and the books are their pillows. A fireplace could be a raccoon home, a place to grow plants, a wastebasket, a hideout, a sleeping place, a rainwater catcher, a stove, a tree holder, a giant's stand-up resting place, a TV corner, and so on.

Use these ideas as a good starting place for your child, then ask her what other things around the house could have other uses. She can write down her ideas and illustrate them to share with you later!

Muffin Tin Moments

Muffin tins are versatile tools that can be used in any number of ways, and they're great to use to keep kids occupied while you're on the phone. Put together a bag of small items to keep handy for "muffin tin moments." For example, give your child a handful of coins and use the muffin tin as a coin sorter. Let your child loose at your desk and it might just become your new office supply caddy! Give him a small ball and it's a mini ball toss game. Just keep in mind if you're going to include a small ball, you're better off with a Ping-Pong ball. Those super bouncy balls have a way of turning quiet muffin tin moments into muffin tin meltdowns!

How Do You Stack Up?

Turn a bag of plastic party cups into a feat of engineering! How fast can your child turn those cups into a pyramid without knocking it over? To make things a little more challenging, start off with ten cups to see if your child can stack them to make a pyramid. Then, add two cups and ask her to try again. (Hint: It's going to be harder with twelve. That's because it's not a "triangle number," which means you can't build a pyramid in which each row has one fewer cup than the row it stands on.)

You can also have cup-stacking races to see who can stack the cups the fastest. Or you can even add a few extra package of cups and have your child build a cup fort!

Making a Movie

With a mobile device and some imagination, your child can make her own short movie for entertainment. She might even want to try using LEGO or action figures to make a stop-motion movie. If she really knows her way around a computer, she can even edit it in a moviemaker program when she's done.

TECH IT UP A NOTCH

Hopscotch HD

This app will have your child dragging and dropping code blocks before you know it! He'll put those blocks together to make games, stories, animations, and even interactive art. (iOS, Android)

Water Bottle Bowling

With a collection of empty plastic water bottles and a small ball, your child can create his own home bowling alley. After the initial prep work, the whole set can be easily stored away in a small box or bag for next time.

Help your child to pour a little salt in the bottom of each bottle for added stability. Then he can set up the water bottles in a pyramid. (He may want to use a piece of tape to mark where each one goes.)

VARIATION

Add a glow stick to each bottle, turn out the lights, and let your child enjoy a round of glow bowling.

Hallway Hopscotch

All your child needs to play Hallway Hopscotch is some free floor space and a roll of masking tape. Task her with making a hopscotch grid out of tape. If she's creative, she can even vary the shapes she uses for the grid. Here are the rules of hopscotch for you and your child to review. It's a game she can play by herself, but it's a little more fun if she has a sibling or friend to play along!

- ✦ Choose something to use as a marker. For Hallway Hopscotch, a small stuffed animal or beanbag works well.
- ✦ Throw the marker, aiming for the first space. If it misses, it's the next person's turn.
- ✦ Hop on one foot, hopping over the first square. Jump with both feet in the parts of the grid that have side-by-side boxes.
- ✦ Turn around, hop back, and pick up the marker on the way.
- ✦ Repeat with each ascending number.

By the time your child makes it all the way through the game, she might even be tired enough to read or draw quietly while you finish up your work!

Be a Bubble (W)rapper

You might be surprised how much fun your child can have with a roll of bubble wrap. (You can buy a roll at your local package or office supply store.) Here are a few ideas for bubble wrap fun:

- ✦ Have a fashion show. With a pair of scissors, some tape, and a roll of bubble wrap, your child can create some interesting outfits. You can even roll out the "bubble wrap" carpet for her to walk down!
- ✦ Make a Hallway Hopscotch grid using squares of bubble wrap.
- ✦ Play bubble wrap tic-tac-toe. Use a permanent marker to write an X or O and then pop the bubble.

Keep in mind, though, that the sound of popping bubble wrap may scare your pets. If you're aiming for quiet, you may want to put your child and your dog on opposite ends of the house!

Candy Bar Messages

This is a fun activity, but you have to be prepared for a potential sugar overload once it's over! Buy a selection of interestingly named candy and gum and place them in a Tupperware container. Then give your child a large piece of paper, a marker, and the bag of candy. His mission is to make a message using the names of the candy! It's okay to use variations of the name, too. You may want to include some masking tape so he can cover up extra letters. (For example, he can put a piece of tape over the last "s" in "Snickers" to make the word "snicker.") Here's an example of a message he could write:

Dear Mom,

I hope you won't <u>Snicker</u> at me when I tell you I made a <u>Whopper</u> of a mess in the kitchen. I was trying to use that <u>Whatchamacallit</u> to cook but I'm such a <u>Butterfingers</u> that it slipped right out of my hand. Now there are just <u>Mounds</u> of broken pieces on the floor. I don't have any <u>Extra</u> money until <u>PayDay</u>, but I promise I will take care of it!

Love,

Your Kid

Sunny Day Alert

In the morning, at lunch, and in the afternoon before you get ready for dinner, take the time to have your child measure the length of his shadow on the ground. If he doesn't have a ruler, he can measure it just by "walk measuring" it by going toe to heel.

Maybe he'll be only "two kid feet" at twelve in the afternoon, but six at suppertime. Ask him to note whether the biggest change is from morning to lunch, from lunch to dinner, or from morning to dinner.

Is he stumped as to why his shadow length changes? Point out that in the early morning and late afternoon the sun is closer to the horizon, so it casts long shadows. During the middle of the day, when the sun is high in the sky, he'll notice that the shadows are much shorter.

Appendix

....

PUZZLE SOLUTIONS

CHAPTER 1

CUL8R

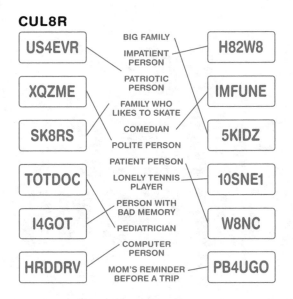

US4EVR	BIG FAMILY	H82W8
	IMPATIENT PERSON	
XQZME	PATRIOTIC PERSON	IMFUNE
	FAMILY WHO LIKES TO SKATE	
SK8RS	COMEDIAN	5KIDZ
	POLITE PERSON	
	PATIENT PERSON	
TOTDOC	LONELY TENNIS PLAYER	10SNE1
	PERSON WITH BAD MEMORY	
I4GOT	PEDIATRICIAN	W8NC
	COMPUTER PERSON	
HRDDRV	MOM'S REMINDER BEFORE A TRIP	PB4UGO

BRAIN TEASER: TRICKY TRANSPORTATION

Their order—four wheels, three wheels, two wheels, and one wheel.

BIG CITY WORD SEARCH

Extra letters spell: Tokyo, Japan, has over twenty-six million people in it. Wow!

BRAIN TEASER: CAN YOU COUNT THE LEGS?
Joey with sixty-eight to Hannah's fifty-eight.

PICKUP TRUCK
Why are sleepy people
like automobile wheels?

B E C A U S E
T H E Y
A R E
T I R E D!

BRAIN TEASER: HOW DOES *X* MARK THE SPOT?
He was using Roman numerals: V + V = X.

BEEP, BEEP

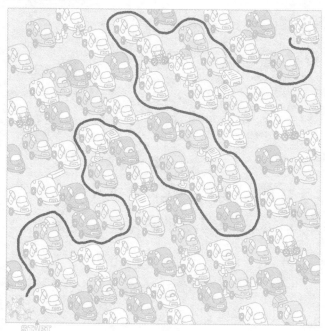

COUNTRY ROAD WORD SEARCH

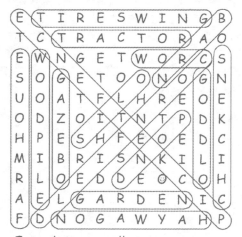

Extra letters spell:
To get to the other side!

BRAIN TEASER: WHICH DOESN'T BELONG?

The Jet Ski—it's the only one that doesn't travel on land.

PIT STOP

You gotta get GAS

BRAIN TEASER: CAN YOU UNLOCK THE ANSWER?

One in 100. Bonus: The odds are twice as good!

BATTY BILLBOARD

TRADER BOB'S BIG
SHOE SALE
THIS INCREDIBLY
SUPER SALE WILL
ONLY LAST A VERY
SHORT TIME.
SHOP FOR SHOES
— NOW!

BRAIN TEASER: CAN YOU FIND THE DIFFERENCE?
The number four

PRETTY POSTCARDS

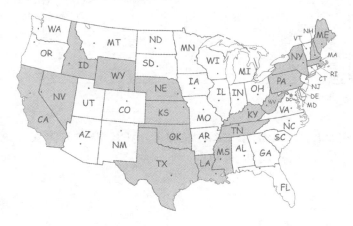

BRAIN TEASER: HOW CAN YOU SEE THROUGH SAND?
When it is heated to almost 3,000°F and the sand becomes glass.

TRASHMOBILE

WHAT DOES THIS STAND FOR?

Save Our Ship

Sealed With A Kiss

BRAIN TEASER: CAN YOU CRACK THE CODE?
I LOVE BRAIN TEASERS.

ON THE ROAD

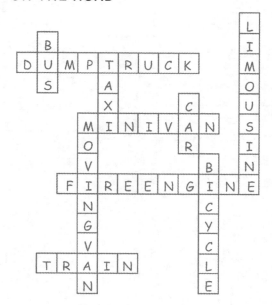

GO! GO! GO!

Not silver = <u>G</u> <u>O</u> <u>L</u> <u>D</u>
Long dress = <u>G</u> <u>O</u> <u>W</u> <u>N</u>
Turkey noise = <u>G</u> <u>O</u> <u>B</u> <u>B</u> <u>L</u> <u>E</u>
Large ape = <u>G</u> <u>O</u> <u>R</u> <u>I</u> <u>L</u> <u>L</u> <u>A</u>
Not hello = <u>G</u> <u>O</u> <u>O</u> <u>D</u> <u>B</u> <u>Y</u> <u>E</u>
A cart = <u>W</u> <u>A</u> <u>G</u> <u>O</u> <u>N</u>
Fairytale lizard = <u>D</u> <u>R</u> <u>A</u> <u>G</u> <u>O</u> <u>N</u>
Didn't remember = <u>F</u> <u>O</u> <u>R</u> <u>G</u> <u>O</u> <u>T</u>
Western state = <u>O</u> <u>R</u> <u>E</u> <u>G</u> <u>O</u> <u>N</u>
Spanish friend = <u>A</u> <u>M</u> <u>I</u> <u>G</u> <u>O</u>
Deep blue = <u>I</u> <u>N</u> <u>D</u> <u>I</u> <u>G</u> <u>O</u>
City in Illinois = <u>C</u> <u>H</u> <u>I</u> <u>C</u> <u>A</u> <u>G</u> <u>O</u>

BRAIN TEASER: HOW WELL DO YOU KNOW THE ALPHABET?

Q, K, nothing.

CHAPTER 2

MOUNTAIN WORD SEARCH

Extra letters spell: It is twenty-nine
thousand and twenty-eight feet tall.

BRAIN TEASER: WHEN DOES THIS FLIGHT LAND?
Seven hours.

STATE YOUR NAME

WEDLAAER	DELAWARE
IOLRAFNCAI	CALIFORNIA
FAIRDLO	FLORIDA
DINOALERDHS	RHODE ISLAND
UTDSOAHTAOK	SOUTH DAKOTA
ZANIROA	ARIZONA
MAAABLA	ALABAMA
WIAIHA	HAWAII
NOTEVRM	VERMONT
SLAAAK	ALASKA
YCEKKUTN	KENTUCKY
ICMNIHGA	MICHIGAN

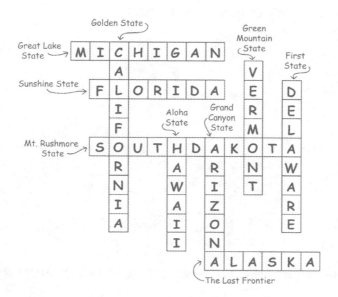

BRAIN TEASER: WHY IS TIME STANDING STILL?
The airplane flew through two time zones.

BRAIN TEASER: HOW CAN THIS BE SO ODD?
Maddy's birthday is on February 29 (it comes only once every four years, in a leap year).

BRAIN TEASER: ARE YOU ON THE RIGHT TRACK?
A train.

ON-THE-GO CHUCKLES

What did
DELAWARE (Dela wear) ?

What did
TENNESSEE (Tennes see)?

What did
IDAHO (Ida hoe) ?

She wore her
NEW JERSEY !

She saw what
ARKANSAS (Arkan saw) !

She hoed her
MARYLAND (merry land) !

OMG, WHAT DOES THIS MEAN?

Hey, this is my work!

Mind Your Own Business

HA, HA, HA!

Laugh Out Loud

BRAIN TEASER: HOW DID SHE ESCAPE?
She cut a hole in the glass with her diamond ring.

BRAIN TEASER: WHY WON'T THIS HOLD WATER?
A sieve.

BRAIN TEASER: SNEAKING A SNACK?
Karl was there at 1:30 P.M., while Kate was there at 1:30 A.M.

GET UP AND GO!
The correct time for the Avion family to get up is 5:45 A.M.

BRAIN TEASER: WHAT INSTRUMENT DOES HE PLAY?

The piano.

CHAPTER 3

• •

A SHORT TRIP

TRAVEL

1. RAVEL   omit "T"

2. REVAL   switch "A" and "E"

3. RELAV   switch "L" and "V"

4. RELAX   change "V" to "X"

BRAIN TEASER: WHO'S ON VACATION?
Nine including the bus driver.

LET'S GET PACKING

1. Call Kelly Short for directions to State park.

2. Buy sun block and bug spray.

3. Check the flashlight batteries.

4. Fill water bottles, make snacks, and get chocolate!

5. Pack ponchos and extra socks.

6. Find binoculars and bird books.

BRAIN TEASER: SOLVE THIS MINI MOTEL MYSTERY
Mini and her family are mice.

HEADING HOME

SEA	SHELL	FISH	HOOK
HORSE	BACK	HAND	BALL
FLY	YARD	OUT	GAME
PAPER	STICK	BREAK	DOWN
BACK	FIRE	FAST	TOWN

START (SEA) / FINISH (TOWN)

BRAIN TEASER: CAN YOU NAME THE WORLD TRAVELER?
The wind.

BRAIN TEASER: THE ROLLER COASTER RIDE
Seven minutes.

BRAIN TEASER: HOW DID THE PLANE LAND?
They used signals.

FAMILY ALBUM

WHAT ARE YOU DOING ON VACATION?

"I can do this all by myself!"

Pick Your Own

What is it?

I don't know, but it's moving fast!

Unidentified Flying Object

BRAIN TEASER: IS THIS A THREE-RING CIRCUS?

Place the first two rings so that one slightly overlaps the other—that's three sections; then, place the third ring in the center of the two, to make seven sections.

AT THE ZOO

BRAIN TEASER: CAN YOU SOLVE THIS ELEPHANT-SIZED PUZZLE?

Six elephants.

CAVE CODE

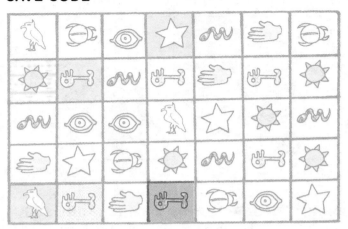

LOOP THE ZOO

Answers: A panda rolling down a hill,
or a penguin stuck in a dryer,
or a zebra chasing his tail!

BRAIN TEASER: WHICH DOESN'T BELONG?
The elephant, because it doesn't have any fur.

WHERE IN THE WORLD

1. Where do fish go on vacation? Finland
2. Where do songbirds go on vacation? The Canary Islands
3. Where do zombies go on vacation? The Dead Sea
4. Where do Thanksgiving birds go on vacation? Turkey
5. Where do geometry teachers go on vacation? Cuba
6. Where do locksmiths go on vacation? The Florida Keys

CHAPTER 4

BRAIN TEASER: HOW MANY PEOPLE CAME FOR PIZZA?
Seven friends (twenty servings minus three for Sara and her parents).

BRAIN TEASER: WHERE SHOULD HE LIVE?
E-Z Street.

BRAIN TEASER: WHEN DO FISH FLY?
Penguins swim; flying fish can fly for short periods of time.

BRAIN TEASER: WHO'S THE MASKED ROBBER?
The raccoon.

BRAIN TEASER: WHAT DOES THE CAT WANT?

"I'm hungry."

SEAFOOD WORD SEARCH

```
S S S A I L B O A T S S
L D E E G D I R B E L
O R R T S H E S V I L
B O E A I L L A G S L
S W S E U K W H A S U
T B H E L G T L S B G
E O Y T S H E Y H E A
R A S A O E A F O S E
P T N U H O R E I U S
O D S U R F E R S L B
T E F I S H E R M E N
```

Extra letters spell:
She sells seashells by the seashore.

HOW HUNGRY ARE YOU?

Bacon, Lettuce, & Tomato

As Soon As Possible

BRAIN TEASER: WHY IS SHE LOSING TIME?

It isn't any farther—it just takes longer.

BRAIN TEASER: CAN YOU READ BETWEEN THE NUMBERS?

You'd get a very full stomach (ate and ate).

FRIGHTENED FOOD

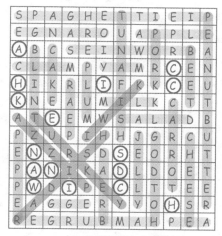

Answer: A CHICKEN SANDWICH

SECOND HELPINGS

SOUP'S ON!

Clam Chowder
Kind of Soup

onions	salt
clams	~~dry sand~~
flour	pepper
~~bathing suit~~	milk
~~plastic shovel~~	~~pebbles~~
potatoes	parsley
~~clam shells~~	~~sunscreen~~
	butter

Chicken
Kind of Soup

water	onion
chicken	~~chicken feed~~
~~chicken wire~~	carrots
pepper	~~grit~~
celery	noodles
~~straw~~	salt
~~egg carton~~	~~feathers~~

Vegetable
Kind of Soup

onions	water
celery	~~watering can~~
carrots	salt
zucchini	pepper
potatoes	~~fertilizer~~
~~glove~~	basil
tomatoes	~~dirt~~
green beans	

CHAPTER 5

BRAIN TEASER: HOW CAN HE EAT SO MUCH?
Each item was a grain of rice.

BRAIN TEASER: THAT'S A HOLE LOTTA FOOD!
Doughnuts, macaroni, bagels, olives, crackers, and Swiss cheese are just a few possible answers.

BRAIN TEASER: WHICH FOOD DOESN'T BELONG?
Tomatoes, because they are a fruit.

WHO PARKED WHERE?

	vehicle	state	color
man with dog	van	Ohio	blue
twin sisters	truck	Maine	silver
family	sports car	New York	red

BRAIN TEASER: HOW DID DAD KNOW?

The moon is not visible every night.

PARKING LOT

A R E   W E

T H E R E   Y E T ?

BRAIN TEASER: WHAT KIND OF FRUIT SALAD IS THIS?

Purple grapes—she was making a fruity rainbow.

BRAIN TEASER: WHAT DOESN'T BELONG?

Spatula.

BRAIN TEASER: THE DIRTY DISHES DILEMMA

It would save him thirty minutes.

BRAIN TEASER: WHAT DO THEY HAVE IN COMMON?

They're all a kind of table.

INDEX

ABOUT THE AUTHOR

AMANDA MORIN (*www.everythingkidslearning.com*) is a parenting and education writer. She also has worked as a teacher and early intervention specialist. She has written for many websites and her parenting articles have been featured on Understood.org, Education.com, KidsActivities.about.com, CircleofMoms.com, and more. She is the author of *The Everything® Kids' Learning Activities Book* and *The Everything® Parent's Guide to Special Education*. She lives in Bangor, Maine.